9th Knowledge Management and Intellectual Capital Excellence Awards 2023

An Anthology of Case Histories

Edited by Dan Remenyi

9th Knowledge Management and Intellectual Capital Excellence Awards 2023: An Anthology of Case Histories

Disclaimer: While every effort has been made by the editor, authors and the publishers to ensure that all the material in this book is accurate and correct at the time of going to press, any error made by readers as a result of any of the material, formulae or other information in this book is the sole responsibility of the reader. Readers should be aware that the URLs quoted in the book may change or be damaged by malware between the time of publishing and accessing by readers.

Note to readers: Some papers have been written by authors who use the American form of spelling and some use the British. These two different approaches have been left unchanged.

ISBN: 978-1-914587-76-4 (PDF)

ISBN: 978-1-914587-75-7(Print)

Published by: Academic Conferences International Ltd, Reading, RG4 9AY, United Kingdom, info@academic-conferences.org

Available from www.academic-bookshop.com

Contents

Acknowledgements

We would like to thank the judges, who initially read the abstracts of the case histories submitted to the competition and discussed these to select those to be submitted as full case histories. They subsequently evaluated the entries and made further selections to produce the finalists who are published in this book.

Dr G. Scott Erickson is Professor and Chair of Marketing in the School of Business at Ithaca College, Ithaca, NY, USA. He holds a PhD from Lehigh University, Masters degrees from Thunderbird and SMU, and a BA from Haverford College. His most recent book, New Methods in Marketing Research and Analysis was published by Edward Elgar in late 2017.

Dr Sandra Moffett is a Professor in Business Analytics and Head of the Ulster University Business School, Ulster University, Magee Campus. Sandra is a core research-active member staff with over 100 high quality, international research publications. She has received a number of research awards and citations for her work.

Dr Anthony Wensley is an Associate Professor Emeritus of Accounting and Management Information Systems in the Department of Management at the University of Toronto Mississauga, with a cross-appointment to the Accounting area at Rotman. He is also the Chair of Communications and Culture and Information Technology Program at the University of Toronto-Mississauga. Some of his research interests include game theory and information systems; intellectual property and knowledge structures; encoding of organizational knowledge; and the understanding, implementing, and managing of enterprise systems.

Introduction

The Knowledge Management and Intellectual Capital Excellence Awards have been held annually for eight years. This year we received 14 case histories for our consideration. After an initial evaluation of the abstracts and full review of the case histories which made it to the second round, we are pleased to present the six finalists in this anthology.

Each of these case histories demonstrate innovative and creative examples of knowledge management or intellectual capital implementation, covering a range of applications including using KM in SMEs, KM in collaboration with AI, knowledge sharing, KM as a means to fostering innovation, KM In the world of micro-finance and sustainability through knowledge management. The case histories this year illustrate a diverse group of ideas from Brazil, Germany, North Macedonia, Morocco, Portugal, and USA

The overall winner of the 2023 Knowledge Management and Intellectual Capital Awards will be announced at the end of the 24th European Conference on Knowledge Management, which is hosted this year by the ISCTE – Instituto Universitário de Lisboa, Portugal on 7-8 September 2023.

Dr Dan Remenyi

August 2023

Intellectual Capital and Knowledge Management at EPIC InnoLabs

Florian Kidschun[1], Ronald Orth[1], Fabian Hecklau[1] and Gábor Nick[2]
[1]Fraunhofer IPK, Division Corporate Management, Berlin, Germany
[2]EPIC InnoLabs Kft., Budapest, Hungary
florian.kidschun@ipk.fraunhofer.de
ronald.orth@ipk.fraunhofer.de
fabian.hecklau@ipk.fraunhofer.de
gabor.nick@epicinnolabs.hu

Abstract: EPIC InnoLabs is an SME based in Hungary that is embedded in an international network of research experts and industry organisations. As a knowledge-intensive organisation, EPIC InnoLabs' organizational set-up is a combination of a research-based foundation and a customer-oriented consulting practice, to support the application of Industry 4.0 solutions world-wide. In order to prepare the organisation for the future, a systematic approach was used to determine the organisation's intellectual capital (IC) and evaluate it in a multi-stage, participatory process. Based on the identified strengths and challenges, a roadmap for the development of the success-critical knowledge and intangible resources in the short and medium-term was designed and implemented. In this paper, the procedure and results of the evaluation of the IC will be presented. Furthermore, implemented solutions are presented and the experiences of the users are reflected upon.

Keywords: Intellectual Capital Statement, ICS, Intangible Resources, Roadmap, Case Study

1. Introduction to the nature of the KM and IC initiative and its specific objectives

EPIC InnoLabs supports companies in creating innovative solutions by conducting research and development work in the industrial environment. Its mission consists in supporting the process of the digital transformation and the implementation of the Industry 4.0 concept with its research, development and consulting services. Its service portfolio covers digitisation, big data analytics, artificial intelligence, with a strong focus on the digital twinning of production, logistics and service systems as well as optimizing the manufacturing and logistic processes.

Within the framework of the Horizon 2020 Project "Excellence Center in Production Informatics and Control" (hence the abbreviation "EPIC"), in the year 2018 EPIC InnoLabs Ltd. was founded as a legally independent non-profit company by Fraunhofer Gesellschaft and the Institute for Computer Science and Control, an affiliated research institute of the Hungarian Academy of Sciences. The central aim of the project was to support the process of becoming self-sustainable by the second half of 2024, by when the newly founded project organization is able to primarily finance its operations through industrial projects which are acquired independently. The company has been supported and developed through the cooperation with two faculties of the Budapest University of Technology and Economics (BME) and four institutions of the Fraunhofer Gesellschaft from Germany and Austria. The venture aims on transferring state-of-the-art scientific results into innovative industrial applications. Currently, new promising technological fields of actuation have been defined, and the service portfolio has been diversified according to market demand.

As a starting point for the business activity, the distillation of key focus products and services and for the development of the IC and KM approach, the value creation model of EPIC InnoLabs was first developed together with the leadership team and other employees and stakeholders. According to Will et al. (2020) the value creation model of EPIC InnoLabs is based on four interrelated components that describe the company's value creation process: (1) intangible resources (intellectual capital, knowledge) are used in (2) business processes (e.g. management of research and consulting projects) that (3) added value to the customer (e.g. optimized productivity) and (4) generate business success (e.g. financial sustainability) for EPIC InnoLabs Ltd. (figure 1).

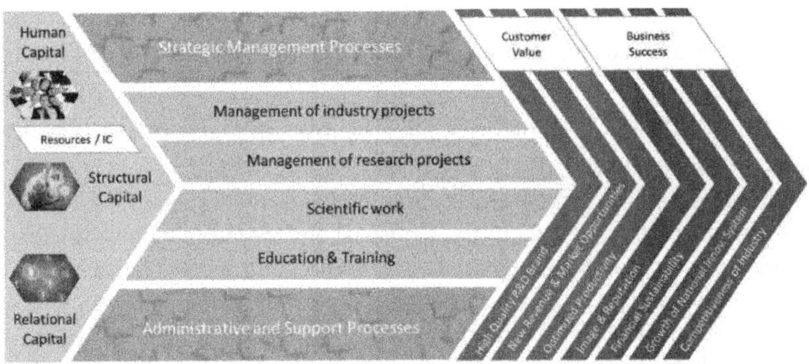

Figure 1: Value Creation Model of EPIC InnoLabs

Intangible resources play a central role for the knowledge-intensive start-up in implementing the business model and achieving organisational goals. Against this background, a participatory approach was chosen in order to better understand these success-relevant factors, to assess the status quo and to plan and manage their systematic development. In a first step, the evaluated method from InCaS (European Commission 2008; BMWi 2008) was used. By using this method, the following advantages can be achieved, which also describe the goals of the initiative at EPIC InnoLabs:

- Diagnosis: analysis of strengths and weaknesses of EPIC InnoLabs' strategic IC factors (SWOT analysis)
- Decision support: prioritisation of fields of improvement with highest business impact
- Optimisation and Innovation: derivation and implementation of actions for EPIC InnoLabs sustainable and organic organisational development (roadmap)
- Monitoring & Risk Management: providing an instrument for controlling strategic risks and measuring success of actions
- Internal Communication: enhancing transparency and employees' involvement through a participatory process
- Reporting: use the results for communicating corporate value to internal and external stakeholders

2. Approach and infrastructure to launch the initiative

The InCaS procedure was implemented within EPIC InnoLabs through a series of workshops with a cross-functional and hierarchy-wide intellectual capital statement team. The procedure as well as the nominated participants' composition together ensure a holistic view of intellectual capital in the organisation.

In order to establish a common understanding among all participants, the first step was to further operationalise the value creation model outlined above by involving the employees and the leadership team. Throughout the process a responsible core team was designing and organizing the series of workshops, as well as supporting the preparation of all employees who were involved in the workshop. The results were visualised in a strategy map (figure 2). In this context, initial target values were also defined in the form of KPIs (e.g. target financing mix in the area of financial sustainability). This result on the overall context provided the corresponding reference and evaluation framework for the further procedure.

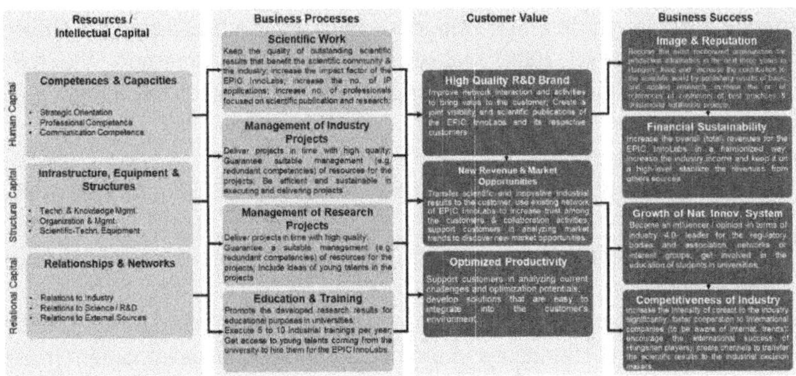

Figure 2: Strategy Map of EPIC InnoLabs

In addition to the overall context, the strategy map also illustrates the significance of IC for business success. The key components of intellectual capital (IC factors) were therefore defined together as part of the process. They form the framework for identifying the success factors needed to launch the initiative. Nine success factors were defined along three IC dimensions as follows:

- **Human Capital:** Strategic Orientation (HC-1), Professional Competence (HC-2), Communication Competence (HC-3)
- **Structural Capital:** Technology and Knowledge Management (SC-1), Organization and Management (SC-2), Scientific-technical Equipment (SC-3)
- **Relational Capital:** Relationship to Industry (RC-1), Relationship to Science and Research & Development (RC-2), Relationship to External Sources (RC-3)

3. The challenges that were encountered, how they developed and how they were overcome

It is of critical importance to know exactly how the intellectual capital (IC) is positioned, as all further steps are built on this foundation. Therefore, grasping the concept of and measuring the IC is crucial for business success. Challenges and deficiencies in the IC that are identified are to be closed through action planning. The overall process from analysis to action planning and implementation was characterised by a participatory approach. For the ICS, 10 people from the company, across all functions were engaged to form the ICS team. They represented all hierarchical levels, including the management as well as the employees and team leaders. An ICS moderator team consisting of two experts from Fraunhofer IPK led the ICS team through the standard

ICS procedure, by moderating, stimulating the discussions with alternative perspectives, documenting the discussions and summarising and evaluating the results. In order to achieve a unified ICS result, regular team meetings and open discussions were necessary prerequisites.

The evaluation of the status quo of the nine IC factors in comparison with the strategic objectives was carried out with regard to the criteria of quality, quantity and systematic on a predefined percentage scale. The assessment results are summarised in the QQS portfolio of EPIC InnoLabs (figure 3). The QQS portfolio provides a profile of strengths and weaknesses. While the x-axis represents the quality of the respective factor, the quantity is represented on the y-axis. The percentage estimation of the systematics for further development is represented by the diameter of the circle. Those influencing factors that are located in the upper right quadrant are well developed. Those that are represented through small circles, especially in the lower left area, show deficits.

Overall, it can be observed that human capital and relational capital are valued less highly than structural capital. In terms of human capital, the factor HC-2 (professional competence) in particular scores poorly in terms of quantity and systematics (too few employees, no systematic HR process). The quality and systematics of HC-3 (communication competence) is also rated as in need of improvement. In the area of relational capital, the factors RC-1 (relationship to industry) and RC-3 (relationship to external sources; e.g. funding agencies, etc.) are not rated as sufficient in terms of quantity and quality. Structural capital is consistently seen as a strength. In particular, the quantity and systematic development were rated well. However, there is potential for improvement in certain areas of quality.

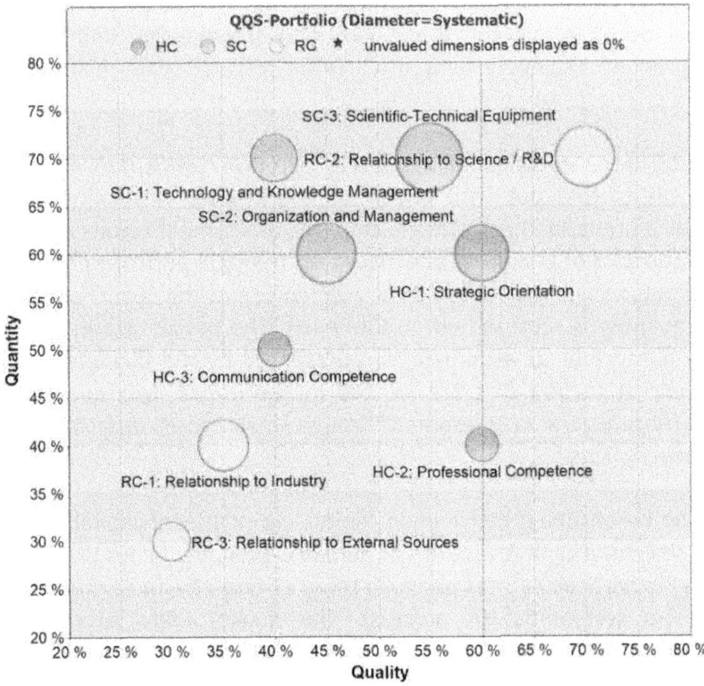

Figure 3: EPIC InnoLabs QQS Portfolio: current strengths and weaknesses

The arguments for the individual assessments were discussed and documented in the workshop team. The central results can be summarised as follows:

3.1 Human Capital

As a result of the analysis we identified that there is a need for people carrying out strategic tasks that support the targeted work towards the vision and mission of the organisation. Our conclusion in this context was that more capacity to focus on strategy development is necessary – employees that possess sufficient strategic competencies are primarily involved in operational tasks. A strategy is in existence, but rather implicit – there is potential for improvement to both formulate it clearly, as well as to effectively communicate it across all functional areas and hierarchies. This underlines the need for regular all-employee meetings (translating business strategy according to changing requirements, strategic business objectives and breaking them down into operational tasks). Professional competencies and technical expertise are to be further developed in accordance with the requirements defined by the strategy. In this regard, we have analysed the level of the competencies for each employee, as well as calibrated the required level of all the competences identified. Afterwards the gap analysis showed the necessary focus on capability development. This analysis and alignment serves as a basis ensuring the achievement of the organisation's strategic objectives, especially in the field of IT development, which is reflected in a rather low quantity result (40%). In this regard, the systematic attendance of training programs and openness to changing requirements of all employees is mandatory. To support this, a training plan was developed through a cooperation of team leaders and the management team. The execution of the training plan was made part of the annual performance setting, to make sure the participants understand the significance of this development area.

3.2   Structural Capital

It became clear that there is a strong need for systematic competitor and market analyses to gain more insights into the concrete market demand for the organisation's solutions. The relevant key competitors have been identified through market knowledge, industry relationships and internet research. Their product offerings, marketing communications and available information on their pricing, and key projects has been reviewed. The management team identified learning points from the competitor analysis. This has also led to conclusions on where EPIC InnoLabs has strategic advantage: which geographical markets are of relevance and interest.

Executing the market analysis, existing products (solutions) have to be systematically matched with industry demands (e.g. collecting ideas to approach potential clients and their problems / demand). Existing tools for acquiring, storing and disseminating knowledge (e.g. cloud, wiki, GitHub) are sufficiently working. However, they are currently not fully integrated, while their handling rarely poses difficulties ('how to use it?'), preventing employees from sharing their knowledge. To gain insights about existing knowledge (e.g. regarding projects), there is no standard procedure in place ('where can I find the information I need?'). This leads to a potential for improvement concerning the documentation and communication of research and project results, as well as a need for regular (mandatory) knowledge sharing meetings. Administrative and support processes need to be clearly defined and systematically developed. One initiative in this respect was the introduction of compulsory internal knowledge sharing meetings which are scheduled in advance throughout the year. The team leaders are responsible for organizing knowledge sharing days. As of today, we see two areas of improvement: the codification of the shared knowledge and the commitment of the participating employees in applying the newly acquired knowledge in their own research (and consultancy) fields.

3.3   Relational Capital

Lots of contacts to SMEs are in existence and aggregated in a CRM database, while the quantity of relationships to large companies is to be improved. This is connected to a potential for improvement concerning the capacity (esp. within sales) for systematic communication (e.g. regular calls) to build up and manage relationships with the industry. Recent developments are going in the right direction: newsletters, events and systematic online marketing activities are implemented. Decent relationships to relevant international R&D organisations are in existence, however there are no clearly defined responsibilities and procedures to maintain and support these relationships. Moreover, the relationships are to a certain extent 'unbalanced': specific partners and organisations are favoured, while others are neglected due to capacity limitations.

4. The learning outcomes that were achieved and how they were measured and evaluated

Based on the identified shortcomings of the gap analysis, an action roadmap for EPIC InnoLabs was created, which outlines the steps the organization should take in the areas of human, structural and relational capital over the years 2021-2023 to improve its overall IC performance.

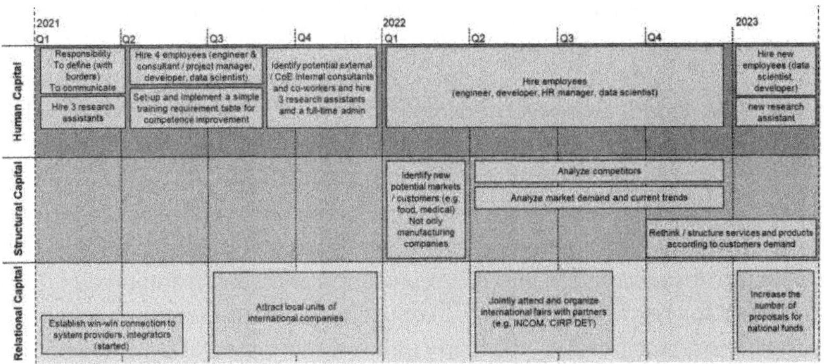

Figure 4: Action Roadmap for EPIC InnoLabs

On the **human capital** level, it became clear that there are too few employees on the one hand and a lack of communication skills and systematic development strategies on the other. Therefore, as shown in Figure 4, a series of recruitment actions were introduced. In 2021, a full-time administrative employee, a developer, a project manager, an engineer and a data scientist as well research assistants (BSc, MSc and PhD students) were hired. In parallel, clear communication responsibilities and training programmes for competence improvement should be established, therefore a PR manager was hired.

Following an initial HR expansion plan, another 5 new colleagues were employed by EPIC InnoLabs in 2022. On the one hand, two colleagues with strong industrial backgrounds, one additional system engineer as well a new data scientist joined the organization. The increased number of employees necessitated the addition of an HR manager to the team. His main tasks include strengthening internal cohesion, implementing a performance evaluation system, as well as an target setting process, and enhancing feedback capabilities for managers. The following table shows the HR expansion during recent years.

Table 1: Employment Development Plans at EPIC InnoLabs Nonprofit Ltd.

Employees (FTE)	2019	2020	2021	2022	2023
CEO	1	1	1	1	1
R&D&I expert	1	1	1	1	1
Project manager	0	0	1	1	1
Consultant, System eng.	2	3	4	5	5
Developer	1	1	2	3	3,5
Data scientist	1	1	2	3	3,5
Administrative, Finance	0	0,5	1	1	1
IT support	0	0,5	0,5	0,5	1
Marketing, PR	0	0	0,5	0,5	1
HR manager	0	0	0	1	1
Research assistants BSc, MSc and PhD students			3	3	4
Total employees	6	8	16	20	23

The organization showed especially a strong need for appropriate systematics to attract, recruit, develop and retain a highly skilled and qualified workforce. To meet this demand, a tailored HR-concept for EPIC InnoLabs was introduced by Fraunhofer IPK, which combines the development of a substantial career plan for specialists and the definition of required competence profiles in order to derive necessary actions, such as trainings or incentives. As a result, the concept helps to implement a HR development concept based on a specialists' career plan.

The first process step focuses on the attraction of employees by suggesting general strategies to provide an attractive working environment for prospective employees. In this context, one of the most important and intensive activities related to the attraction of talents for EPIC InnoLabs constitutes university teaching, at BSc., MSc. and Ph.D. levels. EPIC InnoLabs therefore started regular university courses at various universities in both the cities of Budapest (BME, ELTE, Corvinus University) and Győr (Széchenyi University). To guarantee the recruitment of the right people followed by an appropriate professional development, comprehensive career plans are developed. This includes an academic formation and technical experience profile, the necessary skills and attitude as well as future activities and responsibilities. Based on the career plans, necessary training and qualification programs are derived to ensure a suitable development considering an employee's strengths and weaknesses. At last, it is vital to be able to retain qualified workforce. Therefore, the HR concept contains essential instruments to keep its employees. Identified instruments are for example the introduction of incentives, target agreements, variable salary or recognition strategies.

Based on the HR concept, EPIC InnoLabs continued and further improved their HR activities. Continuing the established best practices, a new employee evaluation and satisfaction process and supporting documentation were developed. The process has been adapted and fine-tuned by considering the best practices from Fraunhofer IPK. The HR evaluation is made now yearly as a standard process with accepted documentation. It contains a table-based self-evaluation and a face-to-face meeting with the management, covering a review the past and planning of the next period, for which both, organizational and personal development KPIs are set. Based on the evaluation, EPIC InnoLabs provides the necessary framework for trainings and further high-level education for the personal development of all employees.

On the **structural capital** level, the strong need to analyse competitors, market demands and current trends have been identified. Therewith, the structure of services and products should be rethought according to the actual market demand. Therefore, a standard procedure for trend scouting, developed by Fraunhofer IPA, was implemented at EPIC InnoLabs. It focuses on identifying technical enablers for the organisation's technology fields and application clusters. Relevant enablers, respectively identified trends and technologies, are described in greater detail in fact sheets that follow a uniform structure. All of them are evaluated qualitatively regarding their overall maturity, as well as their complexity regarding implementation and maintenance. The created knowledge is used as a basis for an internal annual strategy review workshop among the whole EPIC InnoLabs team to prioritize technology fields relevant for EPIC InnoLabs' target market needs in Hungary.

On the **relational capital** level, it was found that valuable relationships with large companies have to be build up. Therefore, in 2021 immediate actions were started to attract local units of international companies and to establish connections to system providers. EPIC InnoLabs became a key member of the I4.0 National Technology Platform Association, which is now one of the major players in the Hungarian I4.0 ecosystem. With its main task of I4.0 strategy formulation, it has a major impact on the directions of I4.0 planning on national level. Furthermore, EPIC InnoLabs, together with further partners, founded the DigiLean Competence HUB, which established itself as a network of more than 1000 entities with the aim to combine the member companies' decades of experience to support the production companies of the domestic industry in their digitization development.

Next to the broad publication of R&D results in esteemed forums of production informatics, the scientific outreach of EPIC InnoLabs and its relations to the scientific community were further strengthened by its increased contribution to international scientific conferences. Here EPIC InnoLabs was one of the organizers of the 17th IFAC Symposium on Information Control Problems in Manufacturing (INCOM 2021), an important forum in the field of smart manufacturing and logistics systems. Furthermore, EPIC InnoLabs acted as a co-organizer of the 10th CIRP sponsored International Conference on Digital Enterprise Technology (DET2021).

5. How the initiative was received by the users or participants

The feedback provided by the management and employees of EPIC InnoLabs was very positive overall. The employees were able to contribute their own experiences, opinions and ideas for the future. Thanks to the inclusive and participatory approach, they were actively encouraged to contribute their own unique experiences, perspectives, and ideas for the organisation's future, which fostered a collaborative and innovative atmosphere during the workshop sessions organized by EPIC InnoLabs.

With the completion of the ICS, the organization has gained in-depth knowledge of the current status quo of its IC. Through meticulous analysis, the ICS team successfully identified and addressed the key gaps, resulting in effective measures that have led to remarkable and enduring improvements. By systematically closing the identified gaps within a short-term action planning approach, strategic objectives set by EPIC InnoLabs were not only achieved but surpassed.

The action roadmap became a central tool for the team to systematically design actions and monitor their implementation. Moreover, to assess the achieved effectiveness, efficiency and competitive advantage outcomes, a control system was constructed following the principles of the balanced scorecard system. This system aids in quantifying and appraising objectives related to the implementation of the ICS.

The overall ICS implementation process facilitated a transformative mind shift of the workforce, empowering them with an increased strategic mindset to further develop EPIC InnoLabs towards its vision. It became clear that knowledge management needs to be interpreted in an increasingly broader sense, as an area where every decision of the company has an impact, and which influences every result and the competitiveness of the company. The most objective measure of corporate success is the feedback from customers and the market. EpicInnolabs is on a path of development, the number of its partners is growing, and its order backlog is increasing year by year, therefore the introduction of the ICS was an important step.

6. Plans to further develop the initiative

For the future development and monitoring of the initiative, it is important to enhance the control of the planned implementations. It is therefore planned to establish a detailed KPI system based on the dimensions set out in the strategy map and the outcomes of the existing balanced scorecard. In addition to such a quantitative measurement, it is also foreseen to repeat the workshop-based evaluation on an annual basis with the involvement of all employees. In this way, EPIC InnoLabs will be able to assess whether implemented measures have brought the desired success, which optimization potential still exists, and how this can be exploited.

Acknowledgement

Work for this paper was supported by the European Commission through the H2020 project EPIC under grant No. 739592.

References

BMWi - Bundesministerium für Wirtschaft und Technologie (Hrsg.). (2008). Wissensbilanz - Made in Germany: Leitfaden 2.0 zur Erstellung einer Wissensbilanz. Berlin

European Commission (2008): InCaS: Intellectual Capital Statement – Made in Europe. European ICS Guideline. Online: www.incas-europe.org

Will, M. (2020): Integrated Strategy Development Based on Intangibles. In P. Ordónez de Pablos & L. Edvinsson (Eds.): Intellectual Capital in the Digital Economy. New York: Routledge. ISBN: 978-0-367-25067-6

Kaplan, R.S., Norton, D.P. (2007): Balanced Scorecard. In: Boersch, C., Elschen, R. (eds) Das Summa Summarum des Management. Gabler. https://doi.org/10.1007/978-3-8349-9320-5_12

Author Biographies

Florian Kidschun, M.Sc. is a researcher at Fraunhofer Institute for Production Systems and Design Technology (IPK), Division Corporate Management in Berlin, Germany. He studied Business Engineering at Technical University of Berlin and Dresden. Since joining Fraunhofer in 2015, he conducted international research & consulting projects in Europe, Brazil and Asia with project responsibility on Strategic Business Development, Benchmarking and Business Impact Analyses. He is the head of the Information Center Benchmarking (IZB) in Berlin.

Fabian Hecklau, M. Sc., studied industrial engineering at the Otto-von-Guericke University Magdeburg and started working in applied research at Fraunhofer IFF in Magdeburg. Since 2015, he works for Fraunhofer IPK in Berlin and is involved in international research and consulting projects in the field of strategic management of organizations and innovation institutions. He is the head of the Competence Center Innovation Systems & Structures at Fraunhofer IPK since 2020.

Knowledge Management during Crises using an Augmented Artificial Intelligence Framework

Mayank Kejriwal

Research Assistant Professor at the University of Southern California Information Sciences Institute

kejriwal@isi.edu

Website: http://usc-isi-i2.github.io/kejriwal/

Abstract: Developed over a period of almost three years, and funded under a federally funded research program in the United States, the Text-enabled Humanitarian Operations in Real-time (THOR) framework was developed with the goal of providing visual and analytical situational awareness to humanitarian and disaster relief planners. THOR was a collaborative effort between industrial and university research laboratories, designed with an intent to support operations in *low-resource linguistic environments* by using semi-automatic Artificial Intelligence (AI) tools to process a rapid deluge of heterogeneous data, including news and social media. Using a visual interface, this processed data is triaged and displayed in an interactive way, allowing operators to gain useful insights without investing much time or cognitive effort. At its core, THOR is powered by a unique knowledge management technology called a *domain-specific knowledge graph*, which is derived from natural language outputs and can be used to efficiently support real-time analytics. THOR has proven its utility on multiple datasets. It has been applied to Twitter data that was gathered in real-time after a major earthquake in Nepal in the mid 2010s, an earthquake from northern China, and the longer-horizon Ebola crisis in Africa. Its research utility has been validated in a range of publications over the last several years, including a demonstration at the prestigious Web Conference in 2018, and several peer-reviewed journal articles and workshop papers. It was also featured as a system in the 60th anniversary of the US Defense Advanced Research Projects Agency (DARPA). THOR serves as an example of how augmented, rather than fully automated, AI can be used for enabling practical knowledge management in difficult situations, and a case study in interdisciplinary fields within computer science and systems engineering coming together in support of solving ambitious and real-world problems.

1. Introduction and Objectives

The United Nations Office for the Coordination of Human Affairs reported[1] that in 2016, more than a hundred million people were affected by natural disasters alone,

---

[1] http://wwww.unocha.org/datatrends2016/WHDT2016.pdf

while over sixty million people were forcibly displaced by violence and conflict. Using interdisciplinary AI research to build a visualization and analytics platform for US civilian and military rescue personnel, as well as the intelligence community, is an important problem with the potential for widespread long-lasting social impact.

The Low Resource Languages for Emergent Incidents (LORELEI) program[2] was established by the US Defense Advanced Research Projects Agency (DARPA) with the explicit agenda of providing situational awareness for emergent incidents, under the assumption that the emergent incident occurs in a region of the world where the predominant language is *computationally low-resource.* Such languages may be quite prevalent in the real world and be spoken by millions of people; however, they are considered computationally low-resource because, within the natural language processing community, tools for processing and understanding such languages may be limited (at least, compared to high-resource languages such as English and French). An example of such a language is Uyghur, a Turkic language spoken by about 10-25 million people in Western China, for which few automated technology capabilities currently exist compared to major Western languages. The cognitive technologies that resulted from LORELEI research were designed to support situational awareness based on low-resource foreign language sources within an actionable time frame i.e., about 24 hours after a new language requirement emerges.

The notion of situational awareness involves far more than machine translation of the low-resource language into English. In addition to offering ordinary natural language processing services, the system must also offer *cognitive* solutions to problems such as entity resolution and provenance reasoning are required to support detailed knowledge management and data analytics for operational use in the field. Entity resolution is defined as the algorithmic problem of linking entities in text or databases that refer to the same underlying entity (Kejriwal & Miranker, 2014). It is known to arise in multiple domains ranging from e-commerce and job posting websites (Balaji et al., 2017; Gheini & Kejriwal, 2019), to human trafficking (Kejriwal & Szekely, 2017a). For example, if the name of a building or address is mentioned in several social media posts, we would not want a system to count them as multiple buildings. Instead, to enable the specialist to manage information effectively, we would want the system to *link* different mentions of these buildings into a single entry, so that the specialist can monitor all relevant information about the situation unfolding in this building in real-

---

[2] http://www.darpa.mil/program/low-resource-languages-for-emergent-incidents

time and in one place (Kejriwal 2014; 2015). Despite having been studied for over 50 years in the AI community (Getoor & Machanavajjhala, 2012; Kejriwal, 2016), entity resolution remains a difficult problem, although recent progress in large language models (such as ChatGPT) have opened up new avenues for the problem.

Similarly, provenance reasoning is described by Townend et al. (2013) as "capturing provenance at source," where provenance of the data includes (but may not be limited to) "where and who it has come from, what time it was created, based on what information, as a result of which decisions or 'value added' operations, and so on." The main reason why provenance is important to users is that, without it, they may find it difficult (or unwise) to trust the data, or any decisions based upon the data. When considering humanitarian and emerging incidents, in potentially volatile regions of the world, it is paramount for users to have some sense of provenance. For example, if the data is coming from a trusted government agency, it is clearly of more value than from an anonymous social media user who may be trying to spread misinformation.

We refer to provenance reasoning and entity resolution as cognitive problems because, even though they are important in the AI community, their primary goal is to minimize cognitive overload for the knowledge management specialist, the first responder and the domain expert who are the target users for such a situational awareness dashboard.

Developing reliable and high-quality algorithms for the natural language processing, and the cognitive, problems, is not adequate in itself. The outputs must also be visualized on an interactive graphical interface, necessarily supporting a human in the loop, as non-technical first responders and field personnel must be empowered to make their own decisions rather than the system being 'trusted' to make the decisions for them. Hence, the system must rely on *augmented* rather than fully autonomous AI technologies (Kejriwal, 2022a). Unlike fully automated AI, augmented AI, just like the name suggests, is meant to augment human beings rather than replace them. Sometimes, the field also goes by the moniker of 'human-machine teaming' and 'human-in-the-loop' systems. However, the latter does not necessarily have to involve AI, while the former applies awkwardly to cases where only one 'human' is involved and the 'machine' is just a graphical interface rather than a physical entity (such as a robot). Hence, we maintain usage of the term 'augmented AI' throughout this case study. As covered in the recent book by Kejriwal (2022b), augmented AI has taken on increasing importance in recent years in a variety of applications (especially within industry) as concerns have arisen about the reliability of purely automated AI.

We designed the Text-enabled Humanitarian Operations in Real-time (THOR) system under the LORELEI program specifically for low-resource languages in the humanitarian and disaster relief domain. Two examples of AI-augmented support by THOR in the are presented Figure 1. The first application is meant to direct the resources of a humanitarian operator to areas that may need immediate attention, while the second resembles classic routing problems in the computer science literature. For the latter application, machine learning modules use both text and entity features to determine (for example) when an area is too dangerous for navigation.

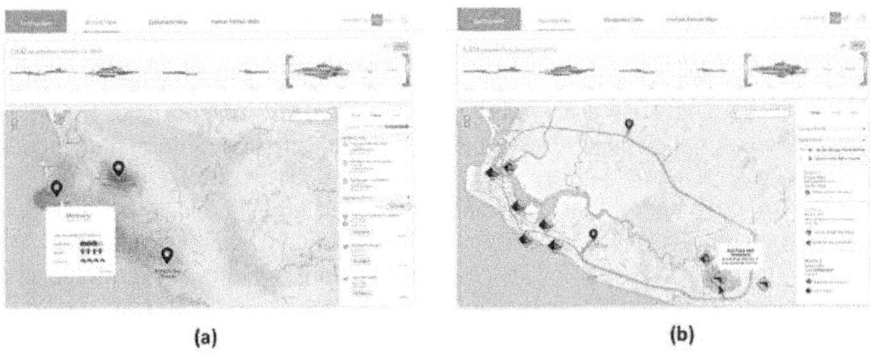

(a)   (b)

Figure 1: Two AI-augmented applications supported by the THOR Graphical User Interface. (a) depicts the hotspots (areas of extreme activity, which may be characterized by extreme sentiments, as well as other anomalies in the data) in a geographical region following an earthquake in Liberia, and (b) depicts a suggested convoy route for delivering much needed water supplies.

Ultimately, THOR is a novel cognitive framework that uses augmented AI to provide solutions to difficult challenges in the humanitarian domain. Figure 2 provides a contextualized illustration of THOR in its overall context. Inputs include streaming corpora of raw documents in a low-resource language (in the most general case) and a set of natural language processing modules collectively denoted as the *language technology development environment* or LTDE that includes state-of-the-art implementations for language-based services such as machine translation, named entity recognition and sentiment analysis. Outputs, which are ultimately shown on a graphical user interface include the two applications just discussed, as well as other interactive utilities for exploring and triaging the data.

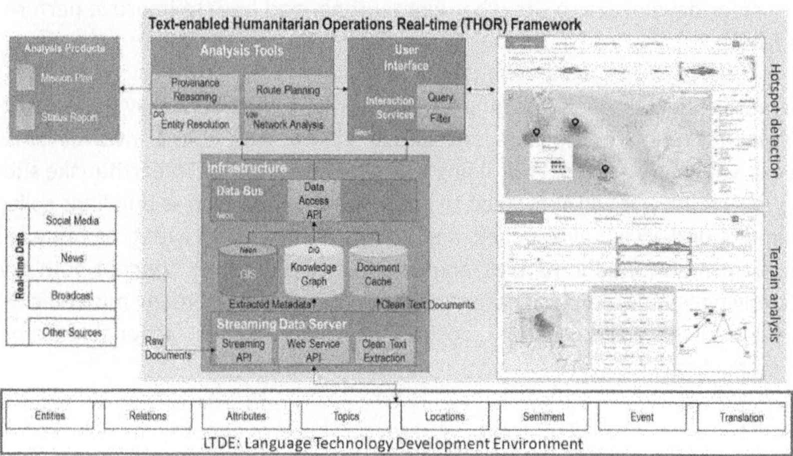

Figure 2: The overall architecture of THOR. Within the streaming data server, real-time data (usually in a computationally low-resource language) is processed using natural language processing modules in the Language Technology Development Environment (LTDE). Extracted knowledge is stored in a semi-structured knowledge graph, and augmented AI tools for network analysis, entity resolution and other analytical tasks, are used to facilitate applications such as hotspot detection, report generation and human terrain analysis.

2. Infrastructure

In this section, we discuss the technical infrastructure of THOR. Because the overall architecture involves many different components (Kejriwal et al., 2018b), we do not aim to provide all technical details in this section. Rather, we outline the premise and rationale of the key modules (visualized in Figure 2) and provide pointers to papers describing these modules in more depth for the interested reader.

First, we note that the LTDE outputs in THOR comprise a combination of unstructured and structured data, as well as metadata, such as the traces of algorithmic executions. Along with such outputs and metadata, both untranslated and translated text fragments are also always retained in the knowledge base so that the end-user has easy access to the original data. In this way, we are able to support provenance reasoning, which is an important requirement in such systems, as described earlier. Trace executions of algorithms are important to retain because, if the higher-level AI modules (such as the natural language processing modules in the LTDE), do not perform at the required level in a given low-resource environment, the traces may allow system developers to see what went wrong, and how to improve performance in the future.

In the most general case, a relevant LTDE-annotated document may be thought of as a *sub-event frame*. At the highest level of abstraction, THOR involves emergent incidents, which are a type of unfolding event. For example, if an earthquake suddenly occurs in a country, it will likely lead to other 'sub-events' such as buildings collapsing, evacuations underway, avalanches, and so on. An unfolding event, as opposed to a single event mentioned in natural language text, is a complex concept both because of its evolving, spatiotemporal nature, and also because of its many micro-facets such as the underlying entity network, socio-political breakdown, actionable items, and social media analytics.

Second, because the LTDE outputs are so heterogeneous, a rich knowledge representation mechanism is needed to support the entire infrastructure (De Nicola et al., 2020). A purely textual database ('corpus') is not adequate as many of the LTDE outputs (such as the extracted entities) are structured. For the same reason, a rigidly structured knowledge representation (such as an SQL or relational database) is also not appropriate. Instead, we opt for a semi-structured knowledge representation using the previously published *Domain-specific Insight Graph (DIG)* architecture (Kejriwal, 2021a; Kejriwal & Szekely, 2017a) to represent the streaming set of sub-event frames as an interlinked knowledge graph. This knowledge graph is constructed in an 'online fashion' (since data is streaming into DIG as the LTDE processes raw inputs as an emergent incident is unfolding and data is becoming available) and is structured according to an *event ontology* that was designed collaboratively by experts with significant knowledge of humanitarian domains. The ontology is designed to capture the humanitarian domain of discourse, including the LTDE outputs that users of the system can utilize for querying, analysis, and exploration. More details on DIG can be found in (Kejriwal and Szekely, 2017b; 2018a; 2019), while the event ontology was described in (Kejriwal et al., 2018a).

The event knowledge graph, derived solely from LTDE outputs and metadata, may be incomplete and possibly noisy. Particularly, the knowledge graph potentially contains entities that are represented differently but refer to the *same* underlying entity, a problem that we earlier referred to as entity resolution. For robust knowledge graph completion[3], one needs to perform fast and automatic entity resolution at multiple levels of granularity and types, as well as entity linking to canonicalize entities with respect to established knowledge bases like DBpedia and GeoNames (Kejriwal, Knoblock & Szekely, 2021). Fortunately, in prior work, we presented robust and efficient solutions to these problems; see, for example (Kejriwal & Miranker, 2016; Kejriwal, 2021b; Tian et al., 2014). A particularly important problem that had to be solved (at least with certain performance guarantees) was event entity resolution, a technical description of which may be found in (Kejriwal et al., 2018a).

The THOR graphical user interface is designed to enable users to gain rapid insight into an emerging event by multi-faceted exploration of the THOR knowledge graph. A dashboard provides multiple linked views that correlate temporal and spatial attributes of the data with attributes extracted by the natural language processing algorithms in the LTDE. As users filter the data according to their interests by interacting with the visual components, all of the linked components are filtered according to the selected attribute, revealing correlations and patterns that may not have been previously evident. For example, a user can investigate the patterns and perpetrators of civil unrest in a specific town by selecting the appropriate topic from a list and drawing a bounding box around the town on the map. As a result, the timeline will display the number of mentions of civil unrest over time, and the entity display will display the names of people and organizations mentioned in the same text.

Figures 3 and 4 provide case study visualizations, using the current THOR graphical interface on some sample social media datasets to analyze two consequential humanitarian events. The interface supports such elements as timelines, volumetric analysis, spatiotemporal analysis, ordinary keyword search, groupings by types and topics, and word clouds.

---

[3] Depending on the domain and data, multiple other steps may be required as well; see, for example, (Kejriwal et al., 2015; Kejriwal, Sequeda & Lopez, 2019; Kejriwal, 2021; Kejriwal, 2022c; Zhang et al., 2018).

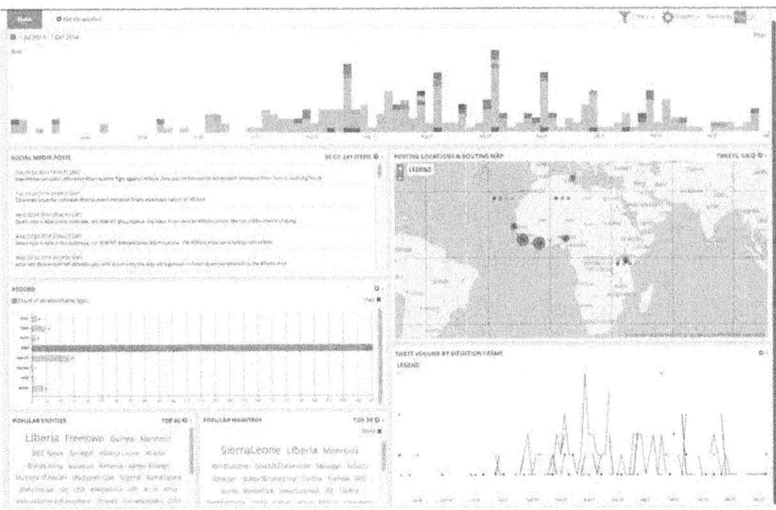

Figure 3: A case study visualization, describing an Ebola outbreak, from the graphical user interface currently supported in THOR. The data shown in this figure is real-world.

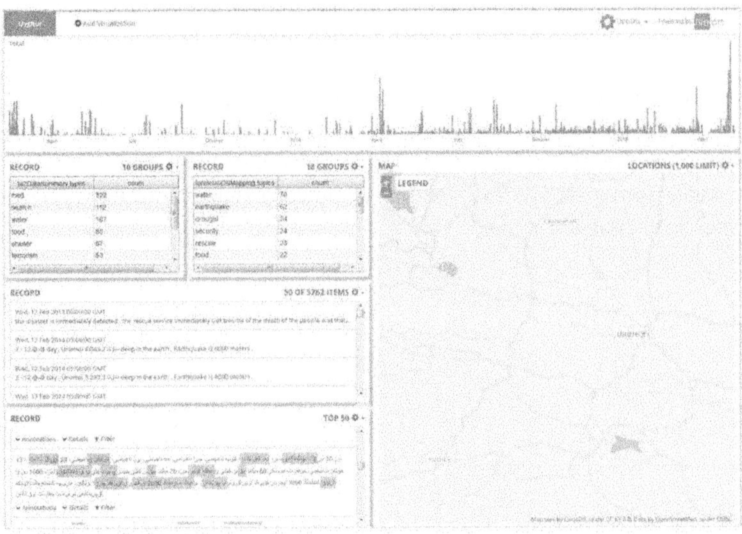

Figure 4: A case study visualization, describing an earthquake in China, from the graphical user interface currently supported in THOR. The data shown in this figure is real-world.

In addition, all text mentioning the person as well as locations mentioned in the text are displayed in a separate *entity-centric search* interface in Figure 5. Entity-centric search is an advanced form of information retrieval that, as the name suggests, seeks to retrieve all available information about an entity of interest (Zhou, 2014). For example, in Figure 5, information about a *person*-type entity is displayed on a single screen. Therefore, rather than retrieve information about this entity in a piecemeal fashion, a user could search for the entity in the dashboard. Any concept (or entity-type) in THOR's underlying event ontology can be retrieved and visualized using entity-centric search. Examples of common concepts include people, places, geopolitical entities, and even events. Good entity-centric search relies on robust algorithms and pipelines for information extraction, which need to be included in the LTDE. In prior work, we discuss semi-automatic implementations and techniques underlying such algorithms (Kejriwal & Szekely, 2017c; Kejriwal, Shao & Szekely, 2019).

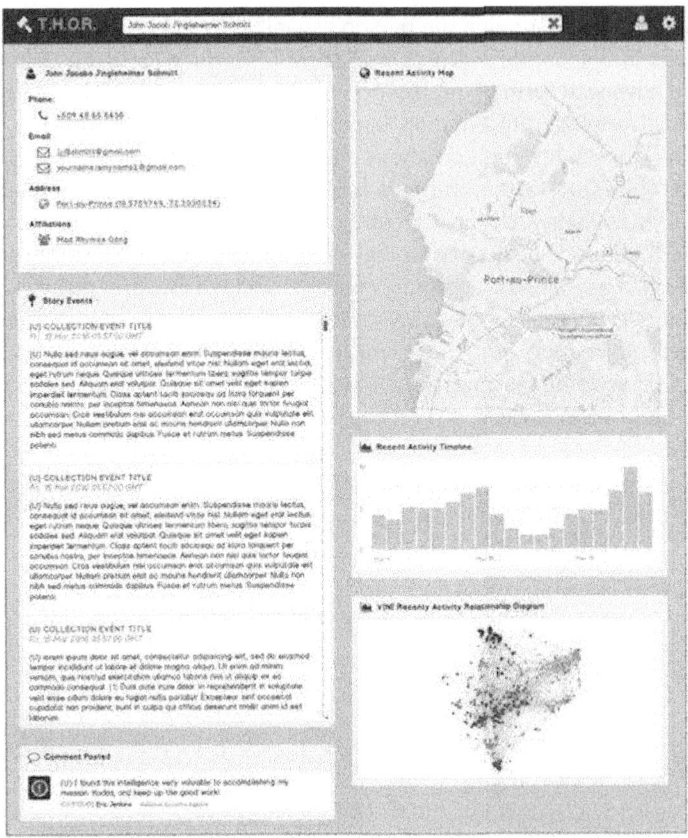

Figure 5: A mockup of the entity-centric search user interface integrated into THOR.

3. Challenges

Because THOR is an augmented AI framework for emergent incidents, especially low-resource languages for which computational tools are under-developed, its development and deployment involved a number of important challenges that had to be overcome before the system could be demonstrated to real users and applied to real datasets. Table 1 enumerates some of the more important challenges. Some of the challenges were engineering-centric, while others were more algorithmic and fundamental.

Table 1. A non-exhaustive set of challenges that an augmented AI framework meant for emergent incidents must generally overcome to be useful to real-world humanitarian and disaster relief (HADR) users.

Systems-level engineering of complex algorithms across the NLP and Semantic Web communities, which can be challenging because many of these algorithms were only tested in lab-settings with many assumptions.
Scale and infrastructure, since a truly comprehensive situational awareness architecture must involve sophisticated query execution over heterogeneous data, including NLP outputs and social media text, images, and hashtags.
Robustness to potentially irrelevant content because much of the data is repetitive, redundant, or even misinformation. Finding genuinely useful information that can then be put on the GUI for a domain expert requires sophisticated information retrieval capabilities.
Presence of missing values and noise, because tweets, text messages and other short-form data that are common in disaster situations and low-resource environments (where strong internet connections may not even be available) often lack context and can be noisy. Piecing together the full picture across many messages and modalities is extremely challenging for any knowledge infrastructure.
Complex query types, since HADR operators may want to retrieve complex types of information (e.g., an optimal route with constraints, a subset of events meeting certain criteria, a ranked list of urgent needs etc.) and the GUI must be able to support those needs.

4. How the initiative was received by the users

THOR serves an integrative role in the overall architecture illustrated in Figure 2, as it provides both the backend infrastructure and LTDE analysis environment for the streaming data processed by the language-based modules, as well as the frontend user interface that is ultimately used to make decisions in the field. Evaluating all of these different facets, while imposing adequate controls, is an ongoing process that requires systems-level collaborations between multiple parties. Central to the evaluations is the provision, collection and annotation of representative real-world benchmark datasets that can be used to evaluate multiple aspects of THOR while studying the effects of such issues as data heterogeneity and error cascading on overall performance. Table 2 provides profiles of some of the datasets that have been collected, either by the LORELEI program or by our own team.

By the time of writing, THOR has already been demonstrated to at least three sets of external users, including for some of the use-cases we illustrated earlier in Figures 3 and 4 (e.g., processing data in Uyghur about an earthquake in northern China, as well as Ebola outbreak in Africa). THOR was also featured in the 60th anniversary of DARPA as an example of a moonshot research system that had found utility among real-world users and organizations. A version of THOR has been demonstrated to personnel involved in field rescue operations in Nepal, as well as organizations like AFRICOM[4] that that are involved in such operations in other regions of the world. We are looking to apply technologies like knowledge graph construction and modeling to COVID-19 data that has been collected over the last several years to demonstrate its potential for pandemic planning in real time, as well as future pandemic preparedness (Kejriwal, 2020). THOR has also been used in a synthetic-data field exercise organized by DARPA in Macedonia to showcase how it could be used when an emergent incident is rapidly evolving. In academia, THOR was demonstrated a few years ago in the premier ACM Web Conference as an example of augmented AI technology for social good (Kejriwal et al., 2018b), and its research has been presented and well-reviewed in both peer-reviewed conferences and journals[5]. More recently, we applied THOR to social media data from southeast Asia, with promising results and feedback from users.

Table 2: Datasets manually collected by our research team to evaluate various aspects of THOR, including entity network embedding and event entity resolution.

Specific Domain/Type of Data	Number of sub-event frames	Time range	Number of unique words	Number of unique named entities
Ebola/Twitter	322,033	2014-07-01 to 2014-10-01	385,305	35,428
Great Britain/Twitter	15,479	2012-10-19 to 2013-02-13	37,181	2,628
Haiti/Ushahidi	3,593	2010-01-02 to 2012-07-03	27,426	3,359
Earthquakes/Twitter	90,853	N/A	53,525	1,830

---

[4] United States Africa Command: https://www.africom.mil/

[5] https://usc-isi-i2.github.io/thor/ contains a partial summary; not including the papers already cited herein, we have also published relevant research, funded under the THOR project, on issues such as efficient and relevant data collection (particularly from social media APIs) (Kejriwal & Gu, 2019), automatic urgency detection in disaster-related text (Kejriwal & Zhou, 2019b; 2020), sentiment analysis (Kejriwal, Fang & Zhou, 2021), and AI methods suited for data and domains with a long-tail distribution (Kejriwal & Szekely, 2018b), among others.

5. Learning outcomes

Because THOR has to take LTDE outputs (especially machine translation), themselves noisy, as inputs, and ultimately outputs interactive user-driven elements, deploying it for front-facing users without a lot of technical expertise can be challenging. Some learning outcomes, especially pertinent to knowledge management, through the development of THOR include:

- When building systems for emergent incidents and disasters, which are necessarily rare and unique relative to each other, the data streams ingested by THOR are sparse rather than high-volume in nature, and need to be further enriched using external knowledge graphs like Geonames and DBpedia.

- It is important to semi-automatically construct such knowledge graphs from raw unstructured data (through processes such as information extraction and clustering), and store them in an appropriate and flexible NoSQL format. We adapted and used the Domain-specific Insight Graph (DIG) architecture (Kejriwal & Szekely, 2019) for representing semi-structured knowledge graphs in THOR. DIG is both flexible and scalable, with many components executable in a Big Data framework like Apache Spark and uses the open-source NoSQL Elasticsearch database for storing the knowledge graph.

- In systems like THOR, scalability can be a minimum prerequisite for engaging users, even more so than accuracy-based performance measures. Because of scalability, open-source data access, as well as ease of setting up high-level analyses, we found DIG to be an appropriate architecture for fulfilling many of the requirements entailed by THOR, particularly graphical interactions with streaming data.

- Similarly, a good graphical user interface is a must for effectively engaging users (Kejriwal & Zhou, 2019a; 2021). The interface must be well designed, and not require much training or customization to set up, even in an old laptop or operating system. As humanitarian organizations cannot really pay for expensive or proprietary software, use of open-source packages is a must.

- Effective solutions to AI problems such as entity resolution can be critical for enhancing the cognitive capabilities of THOR. While classic algorithms can sometimes work for the problem, new algorithmic innovations are often necessary to handle the user and data requirements of the HADR domain.

6. Plans to further develop the initiative

The design of THOR draws on many areas in AI and knowledge management, especially online natural language processing tasks such as named entity recognition, machine learning problems such as topic modeling and sentiment analysis, knowledge graphs, network analysis, entity resolution and linking, provenance reasoning, route planning and graphical user interfaces. Its ultimate goal is to enable humanitarian planners to make decisions in real time without having to worry about the technical 'infrastructure' underlying the system. This has required a careful mix of science, engineering, and practice. Because THOR has so many components, it can potentially be used for domains other than crisis informatics, and humanitarian and disaster relief. Some plans to further develop the initiative include:

- Conduct further user studies, including from organizations that have significant field experience, such as the Red Cross and AFRICOM, to be an effective instrument in the vital mission to minimize loss of life and mitigate the human suffering associated with natural disasters and other calamities;
- Continue to refine the implementation of THOR to make it more scalable while still using open-source tools;
- Use recent advances in language models to improve performance of AI components, such as entity resolution;
- Explore the potential of THOR in other difficult domains like human trafficking, as well as future pandemic preparedness.

We end by noting that a full-fledged THOR graphical user interface is expected to support the various operational goals covered earlier in the introductory section, including dynamic route planning, entity-centric search and visualization of hotspots, sentiments, and entity networks. Of paramount importance is the design and execution of user studies on the interactive aspects of THOR. Constructing benchmarks for evaluating modules such as provenance reasoning are also under discussion.

Acknowledgements

The author gratefully acknowledges the support and funding of the DARPA LORELEI program, as well as Next Century Corporation for developing the front-facing interactive graphical user interface in THOR. Also acknowledged is the aid of partner collaborators and users in providing detailed analysis of humanitarian scenarios, when asked to do so. The views and conclusions contained herein are those of the author, and should not be interpreted as necessarily representing the official policies or endorsements, either expressed or implied, of DARPA, AFRL, or the US Government.

References

Balaji, J., Javed, F., Kejriwal, M., Min, C., Sander, S. and Ozturk, O., 2016. An ensemble blocking scheme for entity resolution of large and sparse datasets. *arXiv preprint arXiv:1609.06265*.

De Nicola, A., Karray, H., Kejriwal, M. and Matta, N., 2020. Knowledge, semantics and AI for risk and crisis management. *Journal of Contingencies and Crisis Management, 28*(3), pp.174-177.

Getoor, L. and Machanavajjhala, A., 2012. Entity resolution: theory, practice & open challenges. *Proceedings of the VLDB Endowment, 5*(12), pp.2018-2019.

Gheini, M. and Kejriwal, M., 2019. Unsupervised Product Entity Resolution using Graph Representation Learning. In *eCOM@ SIGIR*.

Kejriwal, M., 2014. Populating entity name systems for big data integration. In The Semantic Web–ISWC 2014: 13th International Semantic Web Conference, Riva del Garda, Italy, October 19-23, 2014. Proceedings, Part II 13 (pp. 521-528). Springer International Publishing.

Kejriwal, M., 2015, March. Entity resolution in a big data framework. In *Proceedings of the AAAI Conference on Artificial Intelligence* (Vol. 29, No. 1).

Kejriwal, M., 2016. *Populating a linked data entity name system: A big data solution to unsupervised instance matching* (Vol. 27). IOS Press.

Kejriwal, M., 2020. Knowledge graphs and COVID-19: opportunities, challenges, and implementation. *Harv. Data Sci. Rev, 11*, p.300.

Kejriwal, M., 2021a. A meta-engine for building domain-specific search engines. *Software Impacts, 7*, p.100052.

Kejriwal, M., 2021b. Unsupervised DNF blocking for efficient linking of knowledge graphs and tables. *Information, 12*(3), p.134.

Kejriwal, M., 2022a. Augmented Artificial Intelligence. In *Artificial Intelligence for Industries of the Future: Beyond Facebook, Amazon, Microsoft and Google* (pp. 75-100). Cham: Springer International Publishing.

Kejriwal, M., 2022b. Artificial Intelligence for Industries of the Future: Beyond Facebook, Amazon, Microsoft and Google. Springer Nature.

Kejriwal, M., 2022c. Knowledge graphs: A practical review of the research landscape. *Information, 13*(4), p.161.

Kejriwal, M., Fang, G. and Zhou, Y., 2021, December. A feasibility study of open-source sentiment analysis and text classification systems on disaster-specific social media data. In *2021 IEEE Symposium Series on Computational Intelligence (SSCI)* (pp. 1-8). IEEE.

Kejriwal, M., Gilley, D., Szekely, P. and Crisman, J., 2018b, April. Thor: Text-enabled analytics for humanitarian operations. In *Companion Proceedings of the The Web Conference 2018* (pp. 147-150).

Kejriwal, M. and Gu, Y., 2019. A pipeline for rapid post-crisis twitter data acquisition, filtering and visualization. *Technologies, 7*(2), p.33

Kejriwal, M., Knoblock, C. A., & Szekely, P., 2021. *Knowledge graphs: Fundamentals, techniques, and applications*. MIT Press.

Kejriwal, M., Liu, Q., Jacob, F. and Javed, F., 2015, October. A pipeline for extracting and deduplicating domain-specific knowledge bases. In 2015 IEEE International Conference on Big Data (Big Data) (pp. 1144-1153). IEEE.

Kejriwal, M. and Miranker, D.P., 2014, October. On linking heterogeneous dataset collections. In *ISWC (Posters & Demos)* (pp. 217-220).

Kejriwal, M. and Miranker, D.P., 2016. Experience: Type alignment on DBpedia and Freebase. *arXiv preprint arXiv:1608.04442*.

Kejriwal, M., Peng, J., Zhang, H. and Szekely, P., 2018a. Structured event entity resolution in humanitarian domains. In *The Semantic Web–ISWC 2018: 17th International Semantic Web Conference, Monterey, CA, USA, October 8–12, 2018, Proceedings, Part I 17* (pp. 233-249). Springer International Publishing.

Kejriwal, M., Sequeda, J.F. and Lopez, V., 2019. Knowledge graphs: Construction, management and querying. *Semantic Web, 10*(6), pp.961-962.

Kejriwal, M., Shao, R. and Szekely, P., 2019, July. Expert-guided entity extraction using expressive rules. In *Proceedings of the 42nd international ACM SIGIR conference on research and development in information retrieval* (pp. 1353-1356).

Kejriwal, M. and Szekely, P., 2017a. An investigative search engine for the human trafficking domain. In *The Semantic Web–ISWC 2017: 16th International Semantic Web Conference, Vienna, Austria, October 21-25, 2017, Proceedings, Part II 16* (pp. 247-262). Springer International Publishing.

Kejriwal, M. and Szekely, P., 2017b. Knowledge graphs for social good: An entity-centric search engine for the human trafficking domain. *IEEE Transactions on Big Data, 8*(3), pp.592-606.

Kejriwal, M. and Szekely, P., 2017c, April. Information extraction in illicit web domains. In *Proceedings of the 26th international conference on world wide web* (pp. 997-1006).

Kejriwal, M. and Szekely, P., 2018a, April. Constructing domain-specific search engines with no programming. In *Proceedings of the AAAI Conference on Artificial Intelligence* (Vol. 32, No. 1).

Kejriwal, M. and Szekely, P., 2018b, April. Technology-assisted investigative search: A case study from an illicit domain. In *Extended Abstracts of the 2018 CHI Conference on Human Factors in Computing Systems* (pp. 1-9).

Kejriwal, M. and Szekely, P., 2019. myDIG: Personalized illicit domain-specific knowledge discovery with no programming. *Future Internet, 11*(3), p.59.

Kejriwal, M. and Zhou, P., 2019a, August. SAVIZ: Interactive exploration and visualization of situation labeling classifiers over crisis social media data. In *Proceedings of the 2019 IEEE/ACM International Conference on Advances in Social Networks Analysis and Mining* (pp. 705-708).

Kejriwal, M. and Zhou, P., 2019b, August. Low-supervision urgency detection and transfer in short crisis messages. In *Proceedings of the 2019 IEEE/ACM International Conference on Advances in Social Networks Analysis and Mining* (pp. 353-356).

Kejriwal, M. and Zhou, P., 2020. On detecting urgency in short crisis messages using minimal supervision and transfer learning. *Social Network Analysis and Mining, 10*(1), p.58.

Kejriwal, M. and Zhou, P., 2021. Visual Exploration and Debugging of Machine Learning Classification over Social Media Data. *Big Data and Social Media Analytics: Trending Applications*, pp.153-166.

Tian, A., Kejriwal, M. and Miranker, D.P., 2014, June. Schema matching over relations, attributes, and data values. In *Proceedings of the 26th International Conference on Scientific and Statistical Database Management* (pp. 1-12).

Townend, P., Webster, D., Venters, C.C., Dimitrova, V., Djemame, K., Lau, L., Xu, J., Fores, S., Viduto, V., Dibsdale, C. and Taylor, N., 2013, March. Personalised provenance reasoning models and risk assessment in business systems: A case study. In *2013 IEEE Seventh International Symposium on Service-Oriented System Engineering* (pp. 329-334). IEEE.

Zhang, T., Subburathinam, A., Shi, G., Huang, L., Lu, D., Pan, X., Li, M., Zhang, B., Wang, Q., Whitehead, S. and Ji, H., 2018. GAIA-A Multi-media Multi-lingual Knowledge Extraction and Hypothesis Generation System. *TAC, 2*, p.3.

Zhou, M., 2014. *Entity-centric search: querying by entities and for entities*. University of Illinois at Urbana-Champaign.

Author Bioography

 **Mayank Kejriwal** is a research assistant professor at the University of Southern California, and the director of the Artificial Intelligence and Complex Systems research group.

Bringing Novices from the Passive role in Knowledge Sharing to the Active role

Jorge Gomes and Hamid Roham
Lisbon School of Economics and Management (ISEG), University of Lisboa, Lisbon, Portugal
jorgegomes@iseg.ulisboa.pt
hamid.roham@outlook.com

Abstract: Purpose: The nature of firm competition between firms and the source of competitive advantage in many industries has shifted toward a knowledge-based economy. This is particularly the case in knowledge intensive industries, wherein a firm's competitive advantage is highly dependent on its ability to generate and deploy new knowledge solutions. Although knowledge management (KM) is relevant to all organizations, it is likely that its importance is higher at some functional units like maintenance. The field of industrial maintenance is complex and knowledge-intensive. Typically, industrial maintenance knowledge is inaccessible due to industry policies and practices; furthermore, motivation to share knowledge is low or inexistent, due to its tacit and complex nature. Despite these difficulties, sharing knowledge between experienced workers and managers, on one hand, and novices and new comers, on the other hand, is a fundamental problem in industrial maintenance settings, and about which there is still much to be known. The current research reports an investigation aimed at increasing knowledge sharing (KS) between novices and other workers in industrial maintenance. Design/Methodology/Approach: A quantitative field longitudinal research was carried out at a maintenance department of a high-tech company. The research included three steps: the first one assessed the current situation of KM and KS in the department; the second one implemented a number of training programs aimed to increase KS between novices and the rest of the department; and the third one collected information about KM and KS, to assess changes between the two observation moments. Findings: Novices can take an active role in KM and KS in maintenance departments of high-tech industries, rather than a passive role, which can significantly facilitate and improve their own and other employees' knowledge while moderately enhancing the culture of knowledge sharing. Practical Implications: sharing knowledge is a very challenging issue to maintenance managers, faced with risks and problems that need to be acquired by novices. The current research helps knowledge-intensive companies by highlighting solutions that can be designed and adapted to improve employees' knowledge and also KS. Originality/Value: Empowering novices to transition from a passive role in knowledge sharing to an active one, while simultaneously improving their knowledge and also KS practices in industrial maintenance through their involvement.

Keywords: Knowledge management, Knowledge sharing, industrial maintenance, novices, physical asset management, knowledge sharing barriers.

1. Introduction

In today's fast-paced and competitive industrial environment, the importance of KM and KS cannot be overstated (Iheukwumere-Esotu and Yunusa Kaltungo, 2020). Effective KM and KS can help organizations to reduce costs, increase efficiency, improve performance, and achieve a competitive advantage. KM is viewed as an increasingly important discipline that promotes the creation, sharing, and leveraging of the corporation's knowledge (Becerra-Fernandez and Sabherwal, 2014). KM was initially defined as the process of applying a systematic approach to the capture, structuring, management, and dissemination of knowledge throughout an organization to work faster, reuse best practices, and reduce costly rework from project to project (Nonaka and Takeuchi, 1995). Knowledge has been classified and characterized from several points of view to individual, social, causal, conditional, relational, tacit, explicit, pragmatic (Alavi and Leidner, 2001) embodied, encoded, and procedural (Venzin et al., 1998). An important classification of knowledge views it as tacit or explicit (Polanyi and Sen, 2009). Explicit knowledge is knowledge that has been expressed into words and can be shared formally and systematically in the form of data, specifications, manuals, drawings, audio and video, computer programs, patents, and so on (Becerra-Fernandez and Sabherwal, 2014). Among processes of KM, KS has been identified as the most vital one (Asrar-ul-Haq and Anwar, 2016). KS has been identified as the most important process for facilitating organizational learning and innovation and is critical to organizations that wish to use their knowledge as an asset to achieve competitive advantage. The major focus of KS is on the individual who can explicate, encode, and communicate knowledge to other individuals, groups, and organizations (King, 2011).

In the context of industrial maintenance, KM and KS are critical for ensuring optimal performance, safety, and reliability of equipment and systems (Cárcel-Carrasco and Cárcel-Carrasco, 2021). Maintenance is defined as "the combination of all of technical, administrative and managerial actions performed during life cycle of an item intended to retain it in, or restore it to, a state in which it can perform the required function" (Márquez, 2007). The field of industrial maintenance is complex and knowledge-intensive (Aromaa et al., 2015). However, despite the recognized importance of KM and KS, many organizations struggle to implement effective KS practices, particularly when it comes to new or inexperienced employees. Maintenance managers must strongly consider how to transfer expertise and knowledge from experts who have it to novices who need to know (Hinds et al., 2001). An important effect of maintenance KS is that it will transfer maintenance expertise between experts and novices. Novices and newcomers often have valuable insights and fresh perspectives that can contribute to the organization's overall knowledge base, but they may not have the same level of expertise and experience as their more experienced colleagues.

Difficulty in educating and training novices has been identified as one of the most important barriers of KS at maintenance (Chirumalla et al., 2015). To address this challenge, this paper explores a novel approach to KM and KS in an industrial maintenance setting. Specifically, this study has involved novices and newcomers in the KS process by assigning them tasks and using them as lecturers in the presence of experienced colleagues. By doing so, this study aims to facilitate KS between novice employees and their more experienced colleagues.

The paper describes the methodology used to implement this approach, as well as the results and outcomes achieved. It also discusses the implications of this approach for KM and KS in industrial maintenance settings, and provide recommendations for organizations seeking to improve their KS practices. Overall, this paper highlights the importance of involving novices and newcomers in the KS process, and demonstrates a practical and effective approach for facilitating KS in industrial maintenance settings.

2. Method

To embark on this transformative journey of enhancing KM and KS within the maintenance department, the action research methodology was meticulously chosen. This approach resonates with the intricate and collaborative nature of the research endeavor, offering a framework that encourages active participation and iterative refinement.

The study was conducted within a cutting-edge manufacturing organization, which is a subsidiary of a major conglomerate specializing in the production of advanced components for power generation. This conglomerate operates across four distinct plants. The focal company boasts a collection of over 200 modern, sophisticated, and high-tech equipment units, encompassing a wide array of technologies. The maintenance and repair of such diverse and intricate equipment pose significant challenges in terms of complexity, difficulty, and associated costs. At the outset, a robust collaborative effort was undertaken to forge a comprehensive questionnaire. Drawing from established frameworks, this instrument comprised an array of 66 closed-ended questions meticulously crafted to assess the multifaceted dimensions of KM and KS variables. The questionnaire contained 66 closed-ended questions to measure KM and KS variables, and it was administered to 103 maintenance department personnel in mentioned company, which had 1250 employees.

Simultaneously, the involvement of novices assumed a pivotal role in this action research. Fourteen individuals, representing the novice segment, were entrusted with a unique challenge: to construct comprehensive training materials over an intensive two-month span. The scope of these materials was deliberately expansive, encompassing a range of formats spanning Word documents, PDFs, PowerPoint presentations, and engaging instructional videos. Throughout this immersive experience, the novices were thoughtfully supported through a series of four follow-up meetings. These sessions served as collaborative forums, designed to troubleshoot challenges, provide guidance, and harness the novices' untapped potential.

A hallmark of this methodology was the orchestrated pairing of novices and seasoned experts. Guided by sub-department managers, these partnerships culminated in semi-formal training sessions. Herein, the novices, equipped with their diligently crafted materials, assumed the dual roles of educators and learners. This distinctive approach aimed to not only bridge knowledge gaps but also foster a reciprocal and symbiotic learning environment. Accompanying these novices were subject matter experts, adept at their designated domains, imparting precision and depth to the knowledge dissemination process.

Intriguingly, approximately 21.3% of employees were deliberately kept out of the program, serving as a critical control group. This strategic exclusion facilitated a comparative analysis, enabling a robust assessment of the program's true impact on knowledge enhancement and sharing dynamics.

As the five-month program reached its culmination, the research methodology seamlessly transitioned from knowledge acquisition to evaluation. The earlier employed questionnaire was revisited, once again engaging participants to gauge the evolving landscape of KM and KS variables. Moreover, this phase of data collection was infused with an innovative blend of closed-ended and open-ended questions, facilitating a qualitative exploration of participants' experiences. Through their narratives, participants were invited to voice opinions on program intricacies, proffer suggestions for further refinement, and candidly reflect on barriers impeding effective KS.

This multi-dimensional approach also delved into the complex realm of participant roles within the program. Individuals were encouraged to delineate their desired roles, be it as mentors, learners, experts, or a fusion of these identities. This introspective exercise not only enriched program dynamics but also underscored the participatory ethos of action research.

In the quest for comprehensive insights, the evaluation phase further encompassed a nuanced examination of perceived knowledge improvement. Participants were encouraged to quantify the extent of their progress and illuminate the transformative journey they had undertaken. Crucially, the participants' inclinations toward future program involvement served as a litmus test of the program's resonance and efficacy.

The culmination of data collection facilitated a rigorous analysis, fortified by descriptive statistics (using SPSS). This analytical approach unveiled the intricate tapestry of the training program's influence on participants' KS and knowledge augmentation. The holistic perspective garnered through action research provided not only quantifiable insights but also qualitative nuances, offering a panoramic view of the program's impact and the evolving landscape of knowledge enhancement within the maintenance department.

3. Findings and Discussion

The study categorized participants based on their job level, education level, and responsibilities. It investigated the extent to which participants' knowledge improved during the program and the effectiveness of the program in the opinion of various participant categories. The study also examined whether participants across different categories agreed to extend the program. Additionally, the study explored the desired roles of participants in the program, including that of teacher, learner, expert, or a combination of roles.

3.1   Improvement in Knowledge

According to the questionnaire, 67% of learners who attended the program reported an improvement in their knowledge. In addition, 77% of experts and 90% of teachers reported an improvement in their knowledge. Overall, 71% of all participants reported an improvement in their knowledge, and the level of knowledge among participants in the program improved by 43.9%. All participants, regardless of their role (learner, expert, teacher (novice or newcomer)), reported an improvement in their knowledge as a result of their participation in the program. This is particularly noteworthy considering the short duration of the program and the fact that the training was provided by novices. Table 1 presents the percentage of participants who reported an improvement in their knowledge, categorized by the role they played in the program.

Table 1: Knowledge improvement base on the role in the program

Role in the program	Learners	Experts	Teachers (novices and new comers)	Overall
Percentage of participants reporting improvement in knowledge	67%	77%	90%	71%

Table 2 displays the knowledge levels of participants in the taught topic before and after the training by novices. The table is categorized by education level and also presents the percentage of change in knowledge and table 3 shows improvement in knowledge based on position level.

Table 2: Improvement in knowledge based on education level

Education level	Diploma	Associate	Bachelor	Master	PhD	Overall
Average knowledge level prior to Program (scored out of 7)	3.53	3.39	3.52	2.5	6	3.46
Average knowledge level after program completion (scored out of 7)	5.3	5.09	4.86	4.82	7	4.98
Percentage of change	+50%	+50%	+75.5%	+92.5%	+16.6%	43.9%

Table 3: Improvement in Knowledge Based on Position Level

Job level (position)	Technician	Foreman	Expert	Boss	Manager	Director
Average knowledge level prior to program (scored out of 7)	3.34	4.4	3.09	4.37	3.5	2
Average knowledge level after program completion (scored out of 7)	5	5.8	4.27	5	6	6
Percentage of change	+49.7%	+31.8%	+38.1%	+14.4%	+71.4%	+200%

3.2   Effectiveness of the Program (Training by Novices)

Participants were asked to provide feedback on the effectiveness of the program. Table 4 displays the effectiveness of the program based on the job level of the participants, while Table 5 presents the effectiveness of the program based on their education level.

Table 4: Effectiveness of program based on job level (position)

Job level (position)	Technician	Foreman	Expert	Boss	Manager	Director	overall
Percentage of participants who found the program effective	55.1%	80 %	57.1%	62.5%	100%	100%	58.5%

Table 5: Effectiveness of program based on education

Education level	Diploma	Associate	Bachelor	Master	PhD
Percentage of participants who found the program effective	63.6%	56.3%	56.4%	60%	100%

3.3 Agree to Extend (Continuation of) the Program

Participants were asked another question regarding their agreement with extending the program. Table 6 shows the percentage of participants who agreed with extending the program based on their job level (position), while Table 7 presents the percentage of those who agreed based on their education levels.

Table 6. Agree to extend the program based on position

Job level (Position)	Technician	Forman	Expert	Boss	Manager	Director	Overall
Agree to extend the program	56.5%	60%	57.1%	62.5%	100%	100%	58%

Table 7. Agree to continue the program based on education

Education level	Diploma	Associate	Bachelor	Master	PhD
Agree to continue the program	77.3%	59.4%	48.7%	40%	100%

3.4 Desired Roles

Participants were also asked to indicate their preferred role in the program, which included being a teacher, a learner, an expert, or a combination of these roles. Table 8 shows the results for each role.

Table 8: Desired role of participants

Desired role in KM and KS program	Teacher	Leaner	Expert	Teacher and Learner	Teacher and Expert	Learner and Expert	Teacher and (Learner or Expert)	Not answered
percentage	9.7%	50.5%	12.6%	6.8%	1.9%	1.9%	7.8%	8.7%

3.5 Other Findings

The findings of this study indicate that the program has resulted in a modest increase of 3.9% in KS among participants. Additionally, the participants' perception of the culture of KS has increased by 4.6%, but statistically, the difference is not significant. According to the results from the additional questions in the second round of data collection, participants have stated that the main problem with the program has been a lack of motivation. They suggested that the program should be connected and related to their career promotion as an improvement. Interestingly, the control group, who did not participate but were aware of the program, reported an increase in barriers to KS by 12.3%. These results suggest that while the program may have had some positive impact on KS, it may also have inadvertently created new barriers for non-participants.

4. Conclusion

There have been numerous studies on KM in various industrial and service sectors, but typically the focus is on general management, accounting, R&D, development activities, information technology (IT), and similar areas, with less attention given to maintenance units (Cárcel-Carrasco et al., 2020). Within maintenance departments of companies, KM can be challenging due to the tendency of technicians to rely on their own experience rather than sharing and explaining their knowledge of operations (Cárcel-Carrasco et al., 2020).

In this study, the high levels of reported knowledge improvement among learners, experts, and teachers (67%, 77%, and 90%, respectively) suggest that this approach has been effective for a wide range of participants, regardless of their level of experience. This approach has the potential to foster a culture of continuous learning and development, where all employees are empowered to share their knowledge and expertise. Utilizing novices and newcomers as trainers in an industrial maintenance setting has proven to be an effective means of enhancing KM and KS among colleagues. Despite being conducted by novices and newcomers, the trainings have resulted in a significant increase in knowledge for experts, learners, and novices alike, specifically in the area being taught. Moreover, the increase in knowledge is substantial, even though the training was conducted over a short period of time. The findings of this study demonstrate that this approach has resulted in noteworthy improvements in the participants' knowledge, with an overall increase of 43.9% in knowledge improvement. The findings of this study also indicate that the use of novices as trainers has been particularly effective for novices and new comers, with a knowledge improvement rate of 56.52%. This suggests that this approach may be particularly beneficial for organizations that are looking to support the onboarding and development of their new employees. It is also important that most participants preferred to have the role of learner, indicating a need for further investigation to change their attitudes and make them more willing to take on other roles.

One of the most effective ways to learn is by adopting a mindset that allows the learner to teach the material to others. This approach not only helps learners to deepen their understanding of the subject matter, but it also helps them to retain the information more effectively. When learners attempt to teach a concept to someone else, they must organize the material in a way that is easy to understand and follow. This process forces them to break down complex ideas into simple, digestible parts, and helps them to identify any gaps in their knowledge or areas where they need more practice. Moreover, teaching others also requires learners to think critically about the material and consider different perspectives and approaches to the subject matter. By doing so, they gain a more comprehensive understanding of the material and are better equipped to apply their knowledge in practical settings.

In conclusion, the findings of this study suggest that the implemented program has had a meaningful positive impact on the participants' knowledge. Although the increase in KS and culture of KS was not statistically significant, participants reported finding the program effective and agreed to continue it. AS KS is a cultural and multidimensional subject, longer-term implementation of the program may be needed for more significant improvement in KS and its culture. Overall, this study has demonstrated the potential benefits of using novices and new comers as trainers in an industrial maintenance setting. By embracing this approach, organizations can enhance their KM and KS practices, promote a culture of continuous learning, and support the development of their employees.

Implications of the research to the theory and to the practice: This research makes a significant contribution to the theory of KM by emphasizing the importance of KS in knowledge-intensive departments like industrial maintenance, specifically highlighting the involvement of novices in the KM process. By empowering novices to actively participate in KS, the research enhances the culture of KS, improves employees' knowledge, and offers practical solutions for maintenance managers in knowledge-intensive industries. This contribution expands upon existing knowledge by highlighting the active role that novices can play in KS practices. Furthermore, the approach and results of this research hold broader relevance beyond the specific context studied. The methodology and findings presented can be adapted and implemented in a variety of knowledge-intensive companies and departments across different industries. This potential for cross-application demonstrates the versatility and applicability of the research approach, offering valuable insights and strategies to enhance knowledge sharing practices in various organizational settings.

Limitation: The findings of this study are limited by the fact that data were collected from only one company, thus limiting the generalizability of the results. Future research should aim to replicate these findings in other companies to enhance the external validity of the study.

Managerial Implication: Managers can utilize this approach to empower novices by shifting them from the passive side of KM and KS to the active side, while also increasing the knowledge of their employees and enhancing KS.

Future Research Directions: While the outcomes of this study are promising and shed light on critical aspects of knowledge sharing in industrial maintenance, several opportunities for future research deserve attention.

1. Scaling and Generalization: To enhance the practical applicability of our findings, future research could focus on how to effectively scale and adapt the proposed KS approach to various departments and larger organizational contexts. Investigating potential challenges and barriers that may emerge during the scaling process will contribute to a more comprehensive understanding of implementation dynamics.

2. Long-Term Effects on Performance: Further inquiry into the long-term effects of the KS approach on employee development and overall organizational performance is essential. Understanding the sustained impact and potential ripple effects on key performance metrics will provide deeper insights into the approach's enduring value.

3. Program Refinement and Enhancement: To refine and optimize the proposed approach, future studies could engage participants through interviews or surveys. Gathering their perspectives, experiences, and suggestions for improvement would foster a more participant-centric approach, enhancing the program's effectiveness and ensuring it aligns with the evolving needs of the workforce.

4. Addressing Challenges and Limitations: Now, with the inclusion of additional open-ended and close-ended questionnaires in the second round of data collection, the main problems of the program have been identified. As we address and resolve these key issues, the program should continue for a period to allow for the implementation of these resolutions to take effect. Following this, a third round of measurements should be conducted after an interval to assess the impact of issue resolution on the study's results. Furthermore, during this phase, through targeted questions or interviews, the specific contribution of each resolved issue to potential improvements in results can be extracted.

5. Long-Term Sustainability and Adaptation: Exploring the long-term sustainability and adaptability of the KS program over extended periods is another valuable avenue for future investigation. Assessing how the approach

evolves and adapts to changing organizational landscapes and industry dynamics will offer valuable insights into its lasting impact.

In conclusion, these potential future research directions extend the current study's contributions and pave the way for a more comprehensive understanding of KS practices in dynamic knowledge-intensive environments. The iterative approach of addressing challenges, assessing impact, and refining strategies ensures a robust and applicable KS framework for organizations.

References

Alavi, M., and Leidner, D. E. (2001) "Knowledge management and knowledge management systems: Conceptual foundations and research issues", *MIS quarterly*, 107-136.

Aromaa, S., Väätänen, A., Aaltonen, I., and Heimonen, T. (2015) "A model for gathering and sharing knowledge in maintenance work", *Proceedings of the European Conference on Cognitive Ergonomics 2015*.

Asrar-ul-Haq, M., and Anwar, S. (2016) "A systematic review of knowledge management and knowledge sharing: Trends, issues, and challenges", *Cogent Business & Management*, 3(1), 1127744.

Becerra-Fernandez, I., and Sabherwal, R. (2014) "Knowledge management: Systems and processes", *Routledge*.

Cárcel-Carrasco, J., and Cárcel-Carrasco, J.-A. (2021) "Analysis for the knowledge management application in maintenance engineering: perception from maintenance technicians", *Applied Sciences*, 11(2), 703.

Cárcel-Carrasco, J., Cárcel-Carrasco, J.-A., and Peñalvo-López, E. (2020) "Factors in the relationship between maintenance engineering and knowledge management", *Applied Sciences*, 10(8), 2810.

Chirumalla, K., Bengtsson, M., and Söderlund, C. (2015) "Experience reuse in production maintenance: Practices and challenges", *22nd European Operation Management Association Conference*, EurOMA, June.

Hinds, P. J., Patterson, M., and Pfeffer, J. (2001) "Bothered by abstraction: The effect of expertise on knowledge transfer and subsequent novice performance", *Journal of applied psychology*, 86(6), 1232.

Iheukwumere-Esotu, L., and Yunusa Kaltungo, A. (2020) "Assessment of Barriers to Knowledge and Experience Transfer in Major Maintenance Activities", *Energies*, 13(7), 1721.

King, W. R. (2011) "Knowledge sharing", *In Encyclopedia of Knowledge Management, Second Edition* (pp. 914-923). IGI Global.

Márquez, A. C. (2007) "The maintenance management framework: models and methods for complex systems maintenance", *Springer Science & Business Media*.

Nonaka, I., and Takeuchi, H. (1995) "The knowledge-creating company: How Japanese companies create the dynamics of innovation", *Oxford university press*.

Polanyi, M., and Sen, A. (2009) "The tacit dimension", *University of Chicago press*.

Venzin, M., Von Krogh, G., and Roos, J. (1998) "Future research into knowledge management", *knowing in firms: Understanding, managing and measuring knowledge*, 26-66

Author biographies

Jorge Gomes holds the position of Full Professor at ISEG, University of Lisbon, where he imparts knowledge in the fields of HRM, organizational behavior, leadership, and business strategy. His impressive portfolio boasts the publication of over 100 scientific articles and books, including the notable "People Management and Human Capital Manual." In addition to his prolific academic endeavors, he actively participates as a researcher in both national and international HRM projects. Beyond academia, Jorge Gomes extends his expertise to management consultancy, specializing in executive education, organizational change, and development.

Hamid Roham is currently pursuing his PhD in management at the University of Lisboa, Portugal, a journey he embarked upon in 2020. Notably, he obtained his DBA from the same institution in 2020. Hamid's academic journey encompasses an MSc in biomedical engineering from the University of Technology Amir-Kabir, Iran. His research pursuits are centered around the captivating realm of knowledge management and sharing, reflecting his profound interest in these domains.

Fostering Innovation Ecosystems through Knowledge Co-Production: The Case of NAPI Program in Paraná, Brazil

Denilson Sell[1,2,3], Luiz Márcio Spinosa[4,2], Ramiro Wahrhaftig [4], Gérson Luiz Koch[4], Angélica Jung Marques[2,3], Neri dos Santos[2,3], Roberto Carlos dos Santos Pacheco[2,3]

[1]ESAG, Universidade do Estado de Santa Catarina, Florianópolis, Brazil

[2]PPEGC, Universidade Federal de Santa Catarina, Florianópolis, Brazil

[3]Instituto Stela, Florianópolis, Brazil

[4]Fundação Araucária, Av. Com. Franco, 1341 - Jardim Botânico, 82590-300, Curitiba, Brasil

denilson@stela.org.br

spinosa@fundacaoaraucaria.org.br

ramiro.wahrhaftig@gmail.com

gerson_koch@fundacaoaraucaria.org.br

angelicajmarques@gmail.com

neri@stela.org.br

pacheco@stela.org.br

Abstract: Knowledge co-production has been widely discussed in the field of public administration as a means of promoting society's engagement in generating more assertive public policies and promoting sustainable territorial development. In this report, we present the trajectory and results of the implementation of a new model for the development of the innovation ecosystem in the State of Paraná - Brazil, called the New Research and Innovation Arrangements Program (NAPI). The NAPI program is an innovative model that induces knowledge and innovation co-production networks, based on the principles of commons. It focuses on engaging actors in arrangements with defined goals and a shared vision, with the aim of developing solutions to the challenges of the Paraná state. The NAPI program is supported by a digital platform called iAraucária and a knowledge management (KM) strategy that enables the mapping and engagement of actors from the territory in the arrangements for the co-production of innovation. KM, artificial intelligence, and knowledge engineering techniques are combined to promote the articulation of key resources in networks, communities of practice and working groups, connecting the quadruple helix for the development of research and innovation projects aligned with the demands of the territory. Currently, the program has mobilized more than 30 NAPIs, engaging more than 1,300 individuals in collaborative innovation networks. Among the results obtained after three years of implementation, the greater assertiveness of public support for research and innovation stands out, achieving results with a greater potential impact on the sustainable development of Paraná. It is also noteworthy that there been a greater approximation between different types of actors in the innovation ecosystem and a consolidation of research networks in strategic areas for Paraná, as well as the mitigation of risks in the management of the co-production of public policies.

Keywords: Knowledge co-production; Innovation ecosystem; Knowledge Management; Commons; Quadruple helix.

1. Introduction

Socioeconomic development in countries and regions is based on Science, Technology, and Innovation (ST&). In Brazil, Research Support Foundations (RSFs), are important instruments for decentralizing support for ST&I, and are present in all Brazilian states. The 27 RSFs are crucial for local development and aim to promote transformations in regional productive structures through an agenda that includes the training of researchers and the promotion and dissemination of research and innovation.

Regional innovation policies are crucial for both local and national contexts as they foster alignment between innovation, growth, and value creation while acknowledging disparities in resources, culture, and innovative activities across different regions (Shearmur, Carrincazeaux, Doloreux, 2016). In this regard, the Araucária Foundation, the RSF of the state of Paraná - Brazil, performs this role through funding mechanisms and by planning and promoting relational capital at the regional level.

The actions of the Araucária Foundation are operationalized through public or induced calls for research and innovation projects. Its funding flow followed the traditional model, operationalized through calls or request for proposals directed by the government agenda and aimed at supporting projects of individuals or consolidated research groups. However, recognizing that the ST&I system can be viewed as a common good (Hess and Ostrom, 2007), the Araucária Foundation initiated the structuring of a new model to promote research and innovation. This model entails inducing the formation of broad networks, integrating actors and assets from the quadruple helix framework, with the ultimate aim of fostering wealth creation and promoting well-being within the territory.

In this context, the Araucária Foundation has identified three challenges in transforming individual research endeavors into collaborative arrangements that integrate the entire innovation ecosystem. The first challenge lies in comprehending the needs for territorial development through ST&I and identifying the potential for science and technology production in the state. With over 20,000 doctoral degree holders and numerous actors from the quadruple helix framework, along with a diverse range of often unfamiliar assets within the innovation ecosystem (including infrastructure in university laboratories and innovation centers), it is imperative to identify the human and structural capital of the territory in order to allocate resources more effectively. The second challenge relates to the complexity of regional innovation ecosystems, the diversity of actors involved, and the lack of collaboration among them for research and innovation co-production, as well as the sharing of infrastructure and knowledge. Lastly, the intricate nature of ecosystems and the absence of collaboration among actors in research and innovation initiatives pose specific governance challenges for collaborative arrangements.

Acknowledging these challenges, the Araucária Foundation has established a novel model for research and innovation promotion called New Arrangements for Research and Innovation (NAPI). NAPI incorporate elements of the co-production model of common goods (Hess and Ostrom, 2007) to support collective actions that foster innovation and modernization in Paraná. A NAPI is conceived as an arrangement of agents with defined goals and a shared vision, striving to develop a collective and innovative solution through co-production. It represents a regional development model based on ST&I, designed to stimulate knowledge co-production among researchers and other actors within the Paranaense innovation system, driven by priority development demands in strategic sectors for the state.

The NAPI model is anchored in a series of data-driven public calls, aimed at forming networks that integrate actors and assets from the quadruple helix. It relies on a networked co-production model of knowledge and innovation, and its implementation is detailed in the following section.

2. The Infrastructure

The establishment and development of each NAPI follows a process flow, where the stages coalesce the life cycle of a state-funded project with elements that characterize the model as a common. This entire cycle is underpinned by the iAraucária digital platform, as well as various knowledge management methods and techniques.

The flow initiates with demand identification, as illustrated in Figure 1. This can be steered by governmental plan directives, the recognition of latent demands and opportunities via territorial mapping, or through demands identified by nascent quadruple helix arrangements. A comprehensive mapping of intellectual capital information within the territory supports this stage, made possible by the iAraucária platform. Importantly, a NAPI involves collaboration between multiple stakeholders, and isn't designed to address internal management issues within a single organization. Additionally, they employ funding mechanisms from the Araucária Foundation, aligning with the principles of the New Public Services model (Denhardt & Denhardt, 2007).

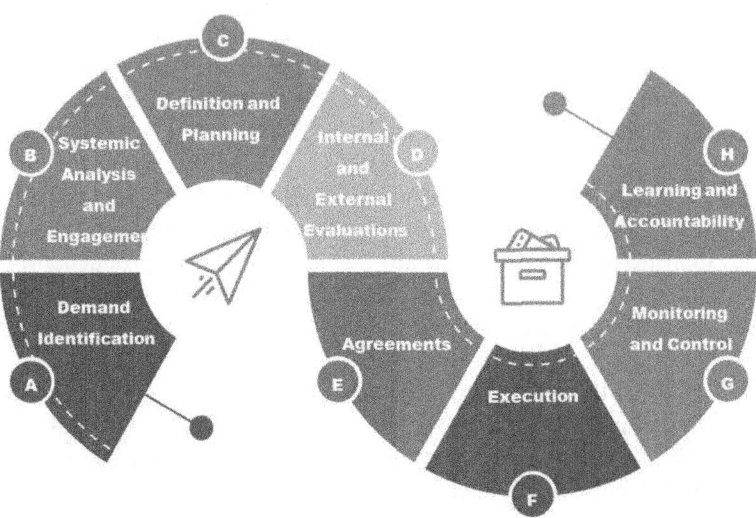

Figure 5: Stages of the NAPI creation and management flow

The stage B of the flow is called Systemic Analysis, which involves deepening the analysis of demands involving a broad discussion about the main factors and movements that are affecting or can affect the ecosystem associated with the future NAPI. This stage may involve the holding of knowledge co-production workshops with quadruple helix actors in which World Café and brainstorming dynamics are applied. The analysis of the ecosystem as well as the identification and engagement of the actors at this stage are supported by the actor and asset location resources of the iAraucária platform.

The stage C characterizes the NAPI. This might involve workshops that mobilize ecosystem representatives who will either lead or support the NAPI's development. Considering that innovation ecosystems depend on knowledge flows that drive collaboration and co-creation to translate this knowledge into added value, the theory of commons provides a basis for establishing the identification of actors and their relations for the co-production of knowledge and innovation in order to manage resources more fairly and sustainably (Marques, 2020). The definition of the NAPI is supported by a Canvas based on the theory of commons covering the elements described in Table 1.

During stage C and progressing into stage D, the management and governance plans for a NAPI are established. At this stage, the principles of commons that can promote the sustainability of the co-production arrangement of knowledge and innovation are addressed, including the definition of mechanisms to promote: i) participation and co-production of knowledge; ii) conflict resolution; c) the application of sanctions and recognition of the actors in the arrangement; d) assessing the reasonableness and proportionality of the initiative; and e) promoting the governance of the initiative (including the delineation of responsibilities, risk management, and monitoring and evaluation strategies of the arrangement actions).

Finally, in stages E, F, and G, cooperation agreements are defined, funding mechanisms are implemented, action, management, and governance plans are executed, and monitoring and evaluation actions of the results are carried out. Ultimately, in the last stage, the lessons learned are assessed, good practices are identified, and the dissemination of knowledge is promoted.

The iAraucária Platform supports all stages of the creation and management flow of NAPIs, with its main modules highlighted in Figure 2. To fulfil this purpose, the iAraucária platform was designed based on knowledge engineering methodologies and ontology engineering (Schreiber et al., 2002), applying principles of knowledge system design and for the representation of knowledge about the themes addressed by the NAPIs.

Table 2: Components of the Canvas for Outlining NAPIs

Item	Description
Value to Society	Mission, vision, and goals
Contribution to Public Policies	Public policies that can be established or strengthened
Identity	Definition and differentiating factors
Target Ecosystem	Breadth, identification of professional and scientific value co-production agents, key agents of knowledge co-production activities, and beneficiaries
Value Proposition	Deliverables, innovation, and knowledge to be co-produced
Channels and Context	Types of relationships and key transactions, and channels for mobilising agents in the co-production and dissemination of knowledge and innovation
Promotion	Promotion mechanisms
Key Activities	Activities that are critical for knowledge coproduction, value delivery and sustainability
Key Infrastructure and Resources	Physical and digital assets, tangible and intangible critical components
Stakeholders	Actors who may impact or be impacted by NAPI or who have an interest in the success or failure of NAPI

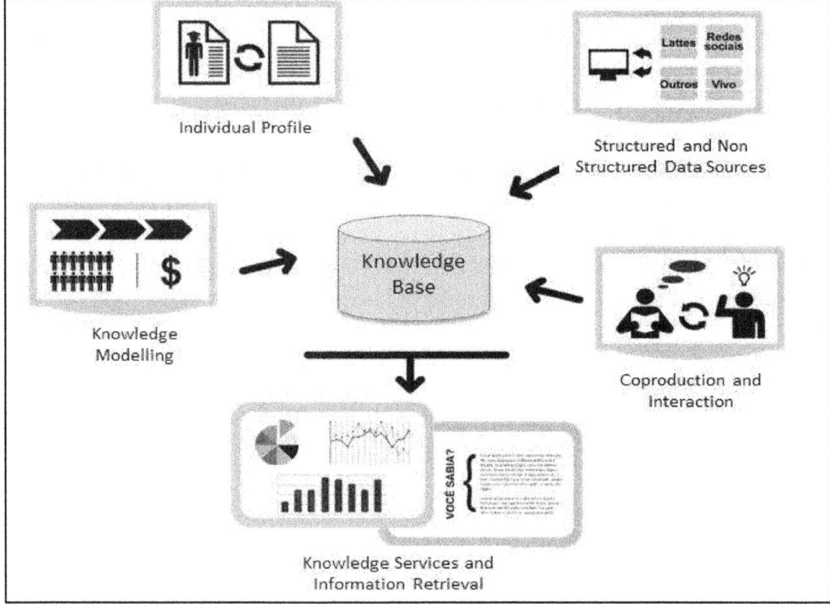

Figure 6: iAraucaria Platform Modules

The iAraucária data bus consists of data from national ST&I databases, such as the curriculum and research groups of the Lattes Platform, gathering information on over 7 million academics and professionals related to CTI institutions, their over 90 million items of scientific and technological production, and about the 46,000 active research groups in Brazil. In addition to these, various data collected from national and international sources characterise the competencies and tangible and intangible assets available in Brazil. Based on the data bus, it becomes possible to analyse the demands and opportunities of the territory (according to stages A and B of the NAPI creation flow) and identify actors and assets to compose the NAPIs and develop co-production actions for research and innovation, thereby supporting all the stages of the flow.

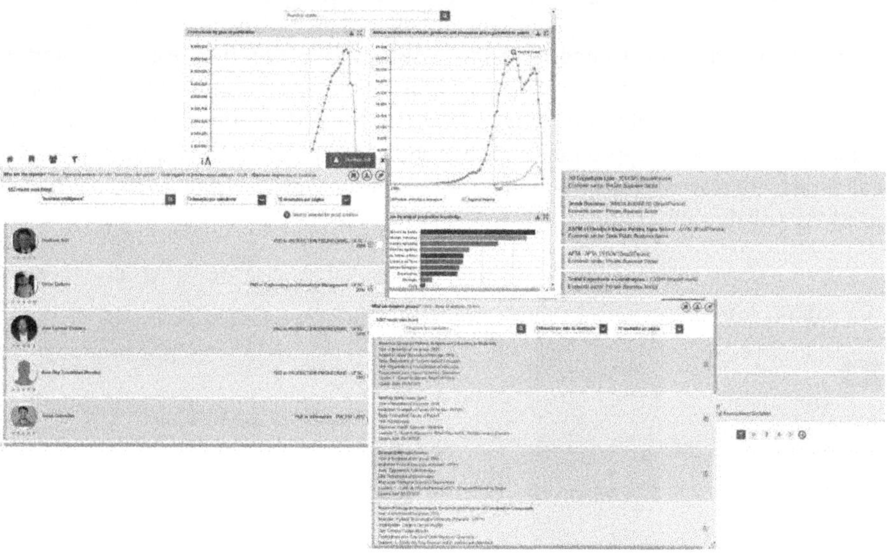

Figure 7: Examples of analytical resources available in the iAraucária Platform to map the competencies and assets of the territory and to engage actors in the actions of co-production of knowledge and innovation of NAPIs

The iAraucária Platform features a structured domain ontology that follows the SKOS standard to describe the prioritised themes in the territory's development, involving topics such as digital transformation, sustainable development, energy, health, among others. The ontology seeks to fulfil the requirements of semantic indexing of the data on the platform's bus, and to support processes of knowledge extraction, recommendations, and analytical processing within the iAraucária framework. Moreover, the platform offers services for registering actors and assets, assisting in the co-production of knowledge, developing NAPI actions, and aiding in the localisation and analysis of knowledge, research groups, institutions, and assets.

Every NAPI set up incorporates a space dedicated to the collaborative development of research and innovation projects. The iAraucária platform promotes collaboration through intelligent support, utilising resources for locating and recommending actors and assets, and fostering engagement for co-production. Its yellow pages resources and location and analysis tools expedite the discovery of expertise and content, thereby facilitating the mapping of opportunities and demands within the territory, and buttressing the knowledge co-production activities within the NAPIs.

In the collaborative environment of the NAPIs, as illustrated in Figures 4 and 5, resources are offered for the localisation of the NAPIs, and to support the discussion, organisation, and distribution of activities in the NAPIs. They also allow the organisation of assets, co-production tools, and content generated through research. At all times, the platform recommends people and content according to the context of the NAPIs' collaborative actions.

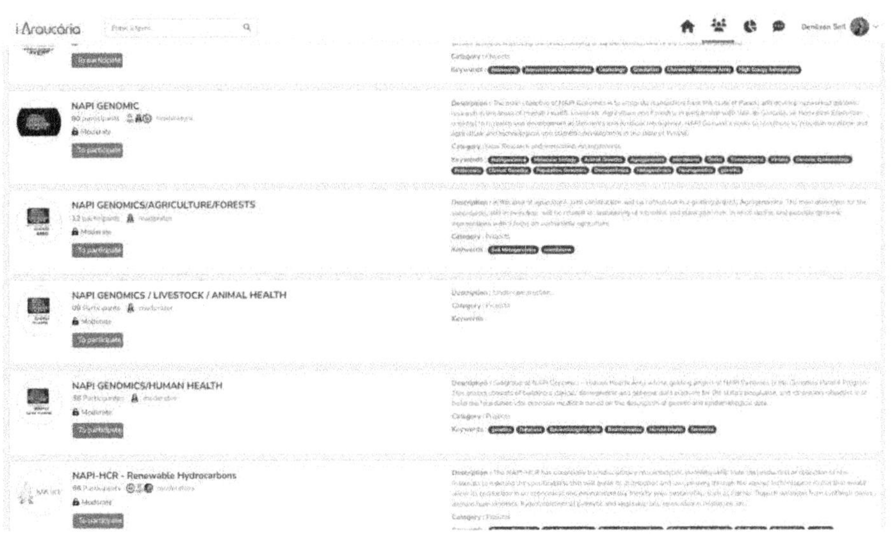

Figure 8: Examples of NAPIs registered in iAraucária

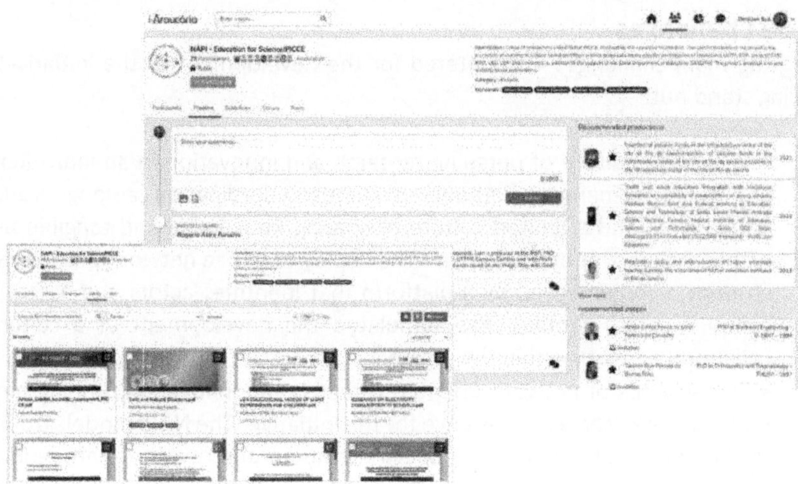

Figure 9: Illustration of resources to support the knowledge co-production

Finally, as illustrated in Figure 6, the iAraucária platform supports the management and governance of initiatives, providing various indicators associated with engagement, collaboration, and achievement of programme results.

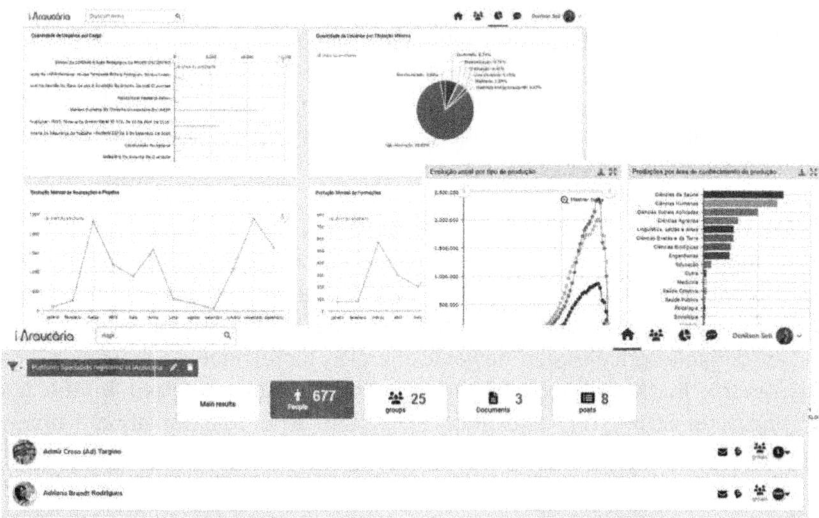

Figure 10: Example of analytical resources to support knowledge management and governance

3. The Challenges

Among the main challenges encountered for the development of the initiative, the following stand out:

- The existing culture of pursuing research and innovation in an individualistic and isolated manner, without substantial coordination among academic participants and a limited culture of sharing knowledge and tangible assets within the innovation ecosystem: The deployment of a network-based funding strategy, supplemented by a platform that identifies actors and assets with complementary profiles, has stimulated the development of a culture of collaborative work within the region.
- • The absence of network-oriented research and innovation funding models that could be used as a reference for the initiative: The NAPI model, grounded in the theory of Commons, underwent numerous revisions throughout its implementation cycle, consistently incorporating lessons learned from initial funding cycles.
- The scarcity of integrated information about competencies, assets, demands, and opportunities within the territory: The strategy of integrating both national and international databases has provided a comprehensive view of the region, thereby fostering strategic funding planning and network coordination.
- The inherent challenges in coordination and communication associated with the inclusion of groups from a variety of educational backgrounds and professional fields: The continual organisation of workshops has facilitated the convergence and exchange of experiences among the diverse actors involved in the NAPIs.

4. How the initiative was received by the users or participants

The NAPI model presents an innovative approach to engaging quadruple helix actors in the co-production of knowledge and innovation and the promotion of the common good. So far, there are 37 NAPIs established or under establishment, covering themes such as sustainable agriculture, renewable energies, biotechnology, education, health, among others. In these, over 1,300 actors have been mobilised in the NAPIs, integrating actors from the innovation ecosystem who traditionally did not work together.

With the aim of identifying the perceived contribution of the NAPI programme, a survey was conducted in October 2022 among actors of the innovation ecosystem. The survey received 1,916 responses, and among the points of contribution and results recognised by the respondents, the following stand out:

- The advancement of the state's ST&I system, earning recognition both nationally and internationally within the ST&I landscape.
- The acknowledgement, leading role, and enhanced integration of diverse actors and valuable assets.
- The bolstering of Paraná's competitiveness through a foundation of ST&I.
- The execution of effective initiatives aimed at promoting wealth and enhancing the well-being within Paraná.
- The valuing of regional governance structures and unique identities.
- The substantial qualitative and quantitative enhancement of ST&I within Paraná's dynamic innovation ecosystem.
- Significant contribution to the 2030 Sustainable Development Goals, with emphasis on those related to education, industry, innovation and infrastructure, health and well-being, economic growth, and sustainable cities and communities.

Finally, it is worth mentioning that the initiative received three awards of high national significance in the ST&I agenda as recognition of the innovative character and high value produced by the NAPI model in Brazil.

5. The learning outcomes

Among the learning outcomes, the following stand out:

- Implementing principles that promote the Commons in the design and operation of NAPIs has been acknowledged as a pivotal factor for the results achieved within diverse constellations of actors engaged in the co-production of knowledge and innovation. In this context, these principles notably facilitate the involvement of various stakeholders, aiding in the comprehension of their unique needs and perspectives, while orchestrating their collective efforts towards a shared ambition for the advancement of prosperity and well-being.
- The proficiency to map, administer, and actively involve diverse participants in innovative co-production arrangements is a quintessential capability for the effective operation of the programme.
- The digital platform, complemented by its robust resources, provides indispensable assistance in managing data pertaining to actors and territorial

assets, fostering collaborative ventures, augmenting actor engagement and interaction, and delineating the state's demands and potentialities.

- Facets of the Commons and knowledge governance have demonstrated their essentiality in building and efficiently managing collaborative innovation networks, providing the groundwork for effective coordination among a myriad of actors in the innovation ecosystem.

6. Plans to further develop the initiative

Future studies will encompass initiatives such as:

- A more in-depth evaluation of the long-term impact of the NAPI program is required to understand the various elements of contribution and whether the benefits observed so far are sustainable over time.
- The integration of new data sources and the promotion of integration with other platforms to expand the coverage of information about the innovation ecosystem, in addition to the exploration of blockchain and AI-based resources to enhance support for co-production of knowledge actions.
- The expansion of the governance and knowledge management strategy to promote closer knowledge sharing between NAPIs and the supplementation of the performance evaluation strategy and network action risk management.

References

Denhardt, R. B.; Denhardt, J. V. The New Public Service: Serving, not Steering. New York: M. E. Sharpe, 2003.

Hess, C. & Oström, E., (2007). Understanding Knowledge as a Commons: From Theory to Practice.

Marques, M. A. J. (2020). Framework conceitual do potencial de coprodução de inovação em ecossistemas de inovação [Tese]. Universidade Federal de Santa Catarina.

Schreiber, G., Akkermans, H., Anjewierden, A., Hoog, R., Shadbolt, N., Velde, W., Wielinga, B. (2002). Knowledge engineering and management: the commonKADS methodology. MIT Press.

Shearmur, R., Carrincazeaux, C., & Doloreux, D. (Eds.). (2016). Handbook on the Geographies of Innovation. Edward Elgar Publishing.

Author Biographies

Denilson Sell is professor of Knowledge Engineering and Management at the Federal University of Santa Catarina and at the State University of Santa Catarina (Brazil). He is also a director at Instituto Stela. He has led several research and development projects with public and private organizations. His most recent work focuses on Knowledge Management, Analytics, Resilience, Digital Platforms and Digital Transformation

Luiz Márcio Spinosa holds a Postdoctoral Degree in Innovation from the University of California at Berkeley (USA), a PhD and a Master's Degree (DEA) in Informatics and Productions from the University of Aix-Marseille (FR). Currently a professor and researcher in the area of innovation ecosystems and knowledge engineering, coordinator of the Research Group National Models and Systems of Innovation of the Triple-Helix Association originating from Stanford University (USA), visiting researcher at the University of California at Berkeley (USA) and Academic and Scientific Director of LabCHIS (Unilivre/UFSC). Since 2019 he has held the position of director of ST&I of the Araucária Foundation.

Ramiro Wahrhaftig is a Civil Engineer graduated from UFPR, with a master's degree in Energy Planning from UFRJ and a PhD in Technology and Innovation at the University of Technology of Compiègne – UTC, France. He interrupted his studies in 1995 to assume the portfolio of Secretary of State for Education of Paraná. He has also been a visiting researcher at Twente University of Technology, the Netherlands, McGill University, Canada, and the University of Texas at Austin, USA. Since 2019 he has held the position of president of the Araucaria Foundation.

Gérson Luiz Koch holds a master's degree in Management Sciences and a PhD in Project Management from the University of Science and Technology of Lille, France. Career employee of the State Secretariat of Administration and Welfare of the State of Paraná, he was administrative director of Paraná Tecnologia (1999-2002), general director of the State Secretariat of Science, Technology and Higher Education-Seti (2002); coordinator of the Management Unit of the Paraná-UGF Fund of Seti (2011-2012). He also held the position of director of the School of Public Management of the Court of Auditors of the State of Paraná (in the periods of 2007-2010 and 2013-2014). Since 2019 he has held the position of Director of Administration and Finance of the Araucária Foundation.

Angélica Jung Marques holds a PhD in Engineering and Knowledge Management from the Federal University of Santa Catarina (2020). He is currently a member of the Research Group on Knowledge Management, Innovation, Interdisciplinarity - KMi2 of PUCRS, and a collaborating member of the research group on Knowledge Engineering applied to Information Management and Organizational Knowledge of the Stela Institute and of the research group on Co-production of Digital Commons, of the Federal University of Santa Catarina (UFSC). She is currently a Technology and Innovation consultant at World Transforming Technologies (WTT Brasil).

Neri dos Santos holds a PhD in Engineering Ergonomics; from the Conservatoire National des Arts et Metiers (1985) - France and a Post-doctorate in Cognitive Engineering from the École Polytechnique de Montréal-Canada. Former President of ABEPRO, Management 92/93 and 94/95. Former Dean of the Polytechnic School of the Pontifical Catholic University of Paraná – PUCPR 2015/2018. He is currently CEO of the STELA Institute and Senior Professor of the Graduate Program in Engineering and Knowledge Management at the Federal University of Santa Catarina (EGC/UFSC).

Roberto Carlos dos Santos Pacheco holds a PhD in Production Engineering (UFSC, 1996) and is a professor at the Department of Knowledge Engineering at UFSC. Participated in the creation and coordinates the Graduate Program in Engineering and Knowledge Management (EGC / UFSC). He was the founding researcher of the Stela Institute. Its academic and technological production results from the co-production with more than 600 collaborators and includes more than 200 publications, as well as software and technical activities of advisory and technical-scientific collaboration. He is currently the leader of the Digital Commons Co-production Research Group.

Knowledge Management in the Micro-Financing Sector: A case of a Network of Knowledge-based Organizations

Nouha Taifi

Industrial Engineering department, Mohammedia School of Engineers, Mohammed V University in Rabat, 10090, Rabat Morocco
Member of the laboratory LERMA, Mohammedia School of Engineers and Coordinator of the R&D Laboratory, ATTADAMOUNE Micro-Finance, Fez, Morocco
nouha.taifi@emi.um5.ac.ma

1. Introduction (to the specific objectives of the initiative)

The small and medium organizations are often the result of investment based on micro-financing support. This latter is one of the most important contributors to poverty reduction and economic development. It is also a strategic actor in social entrepreneurship and social innovation in general; According to (Armendáriz and Morduch, 2005), the positive impact and benefits of Micro-financing is not only shown through storytelling and anecdotes but also through statistical measurement in a global scale and provide interesting cases with longitudinal data and methodological analysis.

The micro-financing sector is one of the most experts sector in business management under less favorable conditions. For this, the interest of management scholars and business practitioners is growing toward the investigation on its strategies of development, collaboration and management. According to Antohi (2009), the micro-financing sector is a social capital for innovation and a strategic social source of local development (Lebossé & Wallace, 1998). Also, it consists of various technological systems for its strategic management (Taifi and Gharbi, 2013); In the case history there are the mention that the information system used usage is ongoing until now year 2023. The administrations from different organizations and competencies in it meet regularly for the management of the network.

The micro-financing institutions that are widely spread in under-developed and developing countries since decades, have competences and expertise in this domain as a result of long-term activities and are further developing managerial and strategic competencies for to be aligned and overcome the challenges of the 21st century paradigms that is urging firms to adopt information and communication technologies and strategic organizational structures of collaboration. In order to continuously develop this social sector, its organizations need to be expert and have competences about the social sector and thus know its characteristics (Sapovadia, 2006).

Besides, concerning innovation management, Tidd (2012) develops on the move of the knowledge management toward strategic competences stating that there are capacities, mechanisms, and routines for innovation;

Therefore, following these various research on micro-financing, the objective of this paper is to present a case study showing the development of the micro-financing sector in which there is the creation of new initiatives. The research paper is mostly at the organizational and managerial levels of investigation. The case study is related to the creation and development of a network of most expert micro-financing institutions and its management in a developing country.

2. The infrastructure, (ie people, systems, exercises, or perhaps hardware, software if any)

The micro-financing institutions in the world are one of the most important actors in economical and societal development. They participate actively in overcoming poverty of the poorest and at the same time continuously support the organizations that are created. They have various success factors as fast adaptation to the environment, efficient MF loans characteristics, efficient and trained staff, and optimal financial processes and systems for the on-going operations of the Micro-financing (Hartungi, 2007). The MF services to their beneficents range from small and medium loans to integration-support in the society (Table 2);

Table 2: The types of micro-financing services

MF services	Description
MF loans	- Loans requested for the launch of a micro, small or medium enterprise or project and their amounts do not exceed the regular bank loan.
Societal integration	- Support to the micro-loans entrepreneurs for the awareness acquisition about the impact of their entrepreneurial initiative as an action to their integration into society.

For instance, the important research of Murisa and Chikweche (2013) on enterpreneurship and micro-finance states that there are challenges to entrepreneurship that has solutions and that MF has great potential to impact on the population. Also, the research of Afrane (2002) makes an impact assessment of MF and find out that MF contributes significantly to business performance and social integration of the population. And, concerning gender MF perspectives on research, there is for instance the research of Nader (2008) stating that MF impacts on the well-being on women and their entire family and thus improves health, education of children, and income, and the research of Ayanwale and Alimi (2004) on gender acquisition of loans from NGOs states that mostly women get higher loans than men to encourage more their enterpreneurial spirit and that incomes are higher for men than women but that in average the income is better than before loan provision.

Also, thus it is clear that the MF engine for development have internal and external actors playing specific roles and taking actions based on specific operational processes and information systems architectures and partnerships; the research of Khandelwal (2007) on the importance of micro-financing institutions, presents their unique characteristics in MF services and their economic benefits compared to regular banking organizations. Thus, these MF engines have thus organizational and operations competencies and capacities leading to the success of their internal environment and their MF services. The micro-financing institutions focus on MF services provision to established types of enterpreneurial initiatives which make this sector an attractive environment for investors.

3. The challenges (how and when they were encountered, how they were overcome)

As entities of collaboration, the organizations in all types of environments have the adequate data, information, and knowledge according to their functions and operations and business purposes in the environment. Thus, they base their activities on not only knowledge residing within the boundaries of their organizations but also on knowledge acquired or shared in an inter-organizational manner through their network of collaborators, partners or co-opetitors. The strategic alliances are important for business performance and innovation since they permit to the firms to react swiftly to market needs (Shan, Walker, and Kogut, 1994; Baum, Calabrese and Silverman, 2000) and to manage the time element that is critical to economic performance and competitive advantage (Yoshino and Rangan, 1995).

The context in which these knowledge-based (KB) and network-based (NB) organizations reside differs from one environment to the other, however, according to Nonaka and Takeuchi (1995) in all cases, through inter-organizational collaboration there is knowledge combination and socialization which shows the objective of network creation (Figure 3). For instance, in the context of micro-financing the managerial practices differences among financial and MF institutions strengthen collaboration among them (Roubos, 2008). Besides, in an economic research in the context of micro-financing institutions and MC-borrowers allocation, Taifi (2004) mentions there are no better method to build capacities in MF institutions than the structural exchange of experience among the practitioners' organizations.

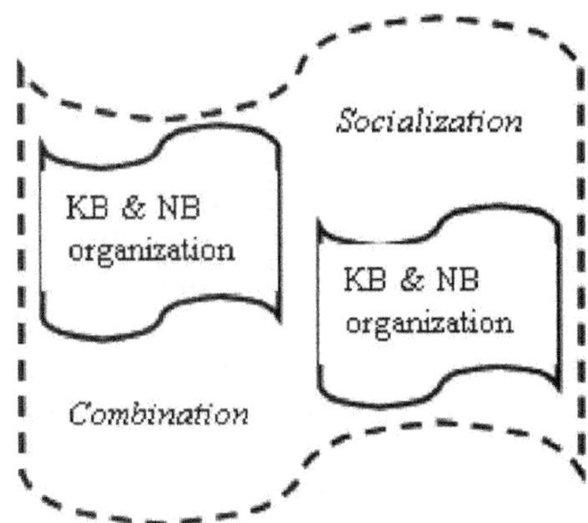

Figure 3: Knowledge sharing within the network

In the context of micro-financing institutions, there are no operational activities without collaboration among various other actors in the environment. In fact, if taken into consideration, the example of funding institutions, supporting MF organizations, show there is inter-organizational collaboration, thus network-based processes (Table 3); for instance, Morton (1997) presents the important role of USAID fundings in providing support for the quality performance of the credit unions in Africa. Also, Alade, Sharma, and Sharma (2003) mention that MF institutions mostly rely on funding institutions and public sources at subsidized rate; it is only in the long-term operations that private funds are reached. Also, for instance, the inter-organizational collaboration of MF institutions with management control or auditing organizations show again a network manner and knowledge sharing process of collaboration (Table 2).

Table 2: The types of micro-financing services

MF services	Description
MF loans	- Loans requested for the launch of a micro, small or medium enterprise or project and their amounts do not exceed the regular bank loan.
Societal integration	- Support to the micro-loans entrepreneurs for the awareness acquisition about the impact of their entrepreneurial initiative as an action to their integration into society.

Thus, in the micro-financing sector, there are network-based and knowledge-based organizations, formed by social entrepreneurs and leading to social entrepreneurship, and various types of networks and knowledge according to the context and objectives of collaboration, and the continuous investigation on their types is more than a strategic topic to further research on. For instance, through a social network analysis, Chen and Krauskopf (2011) research study presents a merger among two non-profit organizations in the micro-financing sector and demonstrate that the executives need to integrate the formal structures but also develop the informal inter-relationships among the human capital of the organizations and to provide them with necessary support for the development of their competences and work activities.

The actual research in this paper would like to analyze and research on a new and larger type of network focus devised by MF institutions. And in fact, for the micro-financing sector is continuously in development, the paper presents a new typology of collaboration adopted in this sector and investigate on its strategic mechanisms and dynamisms. This network formation is also a new type of social entrepreneurship that is expected to bring new social values to the micro-financing sector and resolve various types of issues and challenges in this social sector. Thus, focusing on the organizational, managerial, and strategic levels of investigation, this research framed the following research questions:

- What type of network-based organizations is this? Through answering this question, the research paper aims at the identification of the types of structural ties there are among the members of the network and their functions and roles;
- What are the mechanisms used for its management? This question aims at the investigation on the operations and activities of the network leading to its functioning in an optimal manner;

- What are the strategic dynamisms leading to its success? This question aims at the analysis of the most strategic aspects leading to the success and sustainable development of the network.

4.   How the initiative was received by the users or participants

The creation of this network emerged from the willingless of seven micro-financing institutions to further develop their collaboration and the micro-financing sector. The creation of this network is also supported financially by one of the members of the network that is a banking institution and that has the most strategic players in the grand sister of this network that is a national federation of micro-financing institutions; the members of the network are members of this federation as well. The network headquarter is located in one of the most important MF active regions in this country and has been created in mid-year 2010.

As stated by a respondent, 'the MF financing institutions have each different objectives, resources and capacities', thus, the main objectives of the network is to integrate the information systems among its members and to share strategic data and information about micro-financing so to accelerate the development of the micro-credit small and medium enterprises and to optimize the management of the micro-financing institutions. As stated by a MF institution, 'the objective of the network is to coordinate the activities, to share good practices, and to sustain development', also, another statement is 'one of the objective of the network is to bring support to MF institutions during their interactions with the governmental authorities' or ' the objective of the network is to strengthen the synergies among the MF institutions, to support them in financial funds raising, and to provide mere assistance to MF institutions in crisis phases'.

In more details, the objectives of the network are as follow:

- Standardization of the MF institutions management; that is, the accounting, reporting, financing, and other administrative activities;
- Optimization of each of the seven MF institutions operations through the increase of the quality of the functions and processes and the standardization of the entire management;
- Development of the relationships among the MF institutions through the creation of strong ties among them so to continuously share information, knowledge, and competencies, and be motivated to do that; As stated by one

of the founders, 'the willingness and the participation of the members in the network activities will ensure the development of the network';

- Continuous development of the integrated systems among the members of the network through information and knowledge acquired through the network collaborations;
- Control and monitoring among the members according to their geographical proximity;
- Homogeneous governance and transparency among the members;
- Provision of the right support to the small and medium enterprises as accounting, regulations, and reporting.

The founders of the network have key roles in these seven micro-financing institutions and most of them also have other primary functions in other sectors. According to Ahuja (2000), the partners of the network have different skills and competences and each network' member benefit from the network expertise without extra costs. In the MF network, only 17% of the respondents operate in the micro-financing sector. Their activities in other sectors are academicians, financial executives, consultants, and bank managers and these functions are in the public and private sectors (Table 5) and most of them have long-term active participation in the micro-financing sector; only 17% have less than three years, 33% have less than 8 years and the others have more than 12 years of expertise in this MF sector (Figure 5). The competencies and capacities and knowledge management can become the key factor that lead to the establishment of the network.

Table 5: Respondents' secondary profile in addition to the MF activities

Respondents' secondary profile (private and public sector)	Description
Academicians	Higher education and scientific research and development at higher education institutions, universities and research centers
Financial executives	Financial analysis and forecasting, accounting, auditing…..
Consultants	Analysis and optimization of managerial practices of the organizations
Bank managers	Management of bank accounts, financial analysis and services.

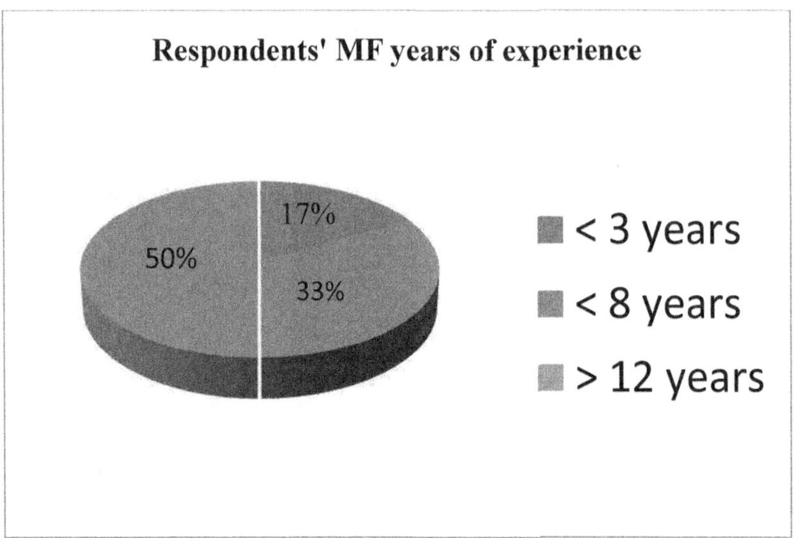

Figure 5: Different years of experience of the respondents' in the MF

The founders of the network have each specific roles and functions in their micro-financing institutions and in the network; in the MF institutions, they are the presidents and within the network, they are the members board, however, only 17% of the respondents consider there is ambiguity in the role played by each MF institutions in the network; that is, there is not a clear understanding about the difference among being a member of the network and a member of a MF institution. The founders of the network and president of their MF institution have the power to delegate functions and missions to members of their MF institutions for the network services or assume them by themselves, however, 33% of the respondents believe there are a lack of consultancy and cooperation in the entire network or 16% of the respondents believe there is a time delay in the achievement of the network creation objectives (Figure 6).

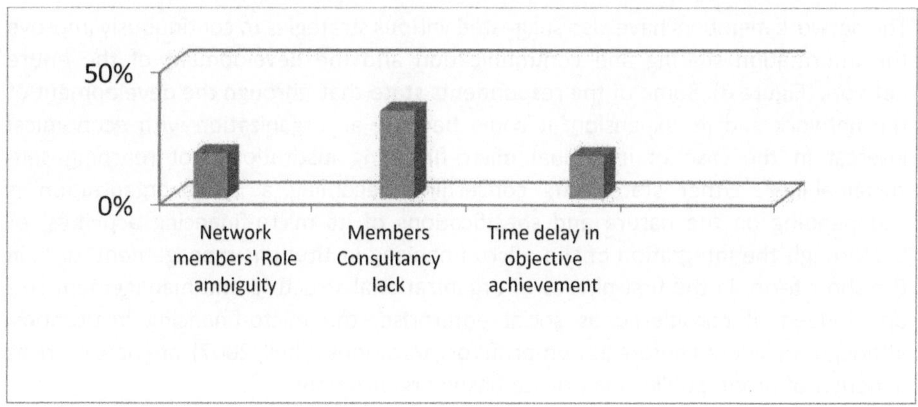

Figure 6: Representation of minor issues of the network

According to Dyer and Singh (1998), managing the network involves using appropriate governance mechanisms, developing inter-firm knowledge sharing routines, making appropriate relationship-specific investments, and initiating necessary changes to the partnership as it evolves while also managing partner expectations. In this MF network, various types of functions and roles in which the board members and their delegates take action; as stated by a MF institution, 'each MF institution have different levels of engagement in the network'. For instance, there is the role of executive director, general secretary, network performance evaluator, external environment – partners-manager, information sharing evaluator, and optimizer.

The information systems of the network are based on various types of communication tools and systems; they are face to face and IT-based interactions (Table 6). The network members organize meetings and seminars and /or share information and knowledge via emails. They also benefit from professional trainings organized when there are new services or products in the micro-financing sector. Besides, an IT-based management information system named SIG is in the phase of development and application within the network so for to accelerate and optimize information and knowledge sharing. The network members are subject to professional training for the understanding and optimal use of the information management system and two network's members already started using it in january and april 2012. Information and communication technologies dedicated to the network organizations are majorly integrated and have specific purposes as to use potential new ways of organizing work activities (Symon, 2010; Taifi and Gharbi, 2012).

The network members have also suggested various strategies to continuously improve the information sharing and communication and the development of the entire network (Figure 8). Some of the respondents state that 'through the development of the network and its expansion, it could become an organization with economical interest in the case of individual micro-financing institutions not reaching self-sustainability'. Other statements concerning becoming a profit organization is '...depending on the nature and specifications of its micro-financing activities' or '.....through the integration of the micro-financing institutions management' or '...in the short-term, in the first phases of organizational structure and management set-up'. Indeed, if considered as social enterprise, the micro-financing institutions, although considered before as non-profit organizations (Chell, 2007), are now more as a merger of profit, public, and private-based organizations.

Besides, as suggestions, the network members perceive the devise of a monthly magazine, report, or newspaper as highly useful so to add another information tool to the information sharing systems of the network and to keep all members updated about new initiatives, products, and services in the micro-financing network and sector. According to Tiwana and McLean (2005), the integration of the expertise and creativity skills of users in the IT-project development phase lead to new products and services innovation. The members of the network also believe it is necessary to have a network website dedicated to the diffusion of the existence of the network on the web, its objectives, and functions and to use it as a support to attract more partners and fundraisers and as a mean for further inter-organizational communication and information sharing among the network members.

Finally, concerning higher strategic decisions-making, 50% of the respondents state the network have capacities and competences to overcome difficult periods of changes in the network as for instance in the case in which individual MF institutions face a crisis phase; For the other half, there are no enough capacities to reach the economic interest. Also, as stated by a respondent, 'as long as each individual MF institution keeps its own identity, management, its own products and have an independent management in the face of crisis of the network, the most important is to recover its database' so to keep information, knowledge, and expertise to remedy to the issues faced. The databases will support the network members in strategic analysis of the most critical situations. Moreover, the creation of this network by itself and the objectives of its inception are a solution to extreme cases to end up with zero-trauma crisis and changes to the MF institutions. According to Franciscus, Koppenjan, and Klijn (2004), uncertainties management in the environment can be through the network approach calling for the development of mutual adjustments and cooperation, and joint decision making for the improvement of problem-solving.

5. The learning outcomes (What was achieved and how the outcomes were measured/evaluated)

The purpose of the study is to further investigate on the network-based and knowledge-based organizations in the micro-financing sector and the social entrepreneurship undergone to activate social and economic performance because the engineering of social enterpreneurship in the micro-financing sector requires new models and approaches. According to Kanter (1999), the social sector is moving toward being a source of innovation and new managerial approaches adoption. Also, Sagaw, and Segal (1999) state that value creation in the social sector arises through business-social sector partnerships. The research focused on the analysis of the mechanisms and dynamisms of a new type of inter-organizational collaboration and its network focus. The results show that this case study have various important objectives, strategic processes, and practices and that it is a continuous innovation network. In particular, the development of social enterpreneurship capacities and actions should be based on knowledge, experience, and methods which make social enterpreneurship a process where its actors as the MFIs and their networks are experts based on sustainable processes of entrepreneurship.

The paper provides a list of guidelines based on the results of the research. The guidelines are the mechanisms and dynamisms leading to the continuous success of the network, and they can be considered as a standard methodology for the management of networks. The guidelines are as follows:

First, the direct ties of the founders of the network are the first pillar for the success of the strategic collaboration leading to homogeneity among the members of the network. The founders must have a multi-disciplinarity background and expertise in the sector for strategic decision making.

Second, the founders and top-management of the network have capacities to delegate to the right person some operations in the network; this choice is based on the background and expertise of the person in charge of the operations and lead to an heterogeneity in active participation.

Third, the level of engagement of the members, also based on the expertise of the members, allow a clear and sustainable strategic positioning and decision making—within the network.

Fourth, the indirect ties among the members represented by the lack of consultancy is also a strategic pillar leading to the involvement of top-and middle management and external actors, and the use of delegation.

Fifth, to allow inception and development of the network, financial and IT-support is necessary so to accelerate organizational structure development and information and communication sharing.

6.   Plans to further develop the initiative

The study contributes to the development of literature on organizational structure development and change and more precisely inter-organizational collaboration. The research further demonstrates the importance and impact of networking on the competencies and operational development, and economic performance. Besides, the research results show that inter-organizational networking can have simultaneously various objectives and strategic processes.

The research also advances theory on the micro-financing sector stating it is a dynamic environment in continuous change and development for it is in possess of capacities and competencies for innovation and knowledge creation; this contributes to innovation management discipline as well. Also, the study, based on the results, states the micro-financing sector have strategic managerial methodologies leading to its continuous success; this contributes to the entire management science disciplines.

References

Afrane, S. (2002), Impact assessment of microfinance interventions in Ghana and South Africa: A synthesis of major impacts and lessons, Journal of Microfinance, Vol. 4, N. 1, pp. 37-58.

Alade, J.A., Sharma, D.K. and Sharma, H.P. (2003), The role of microenterprise finance in economic development, Journal of Academy of Business and Economics, Vol.1, Issue: 1.

Armendáriz, B and Morduch, J. (2005), The Economics of Microfinance, The MIT Press: Cambridge, Massachusetts.

Antohi, M. (2009), *Microfinance, capital for innovation*, in: MacCallum, D., Moulaert, F., Hillier, J. And Haddock, S.V. (eds), Social innovation and territorial development, chp 3, pp. 39-62. Farnham, England and Burlington, USA: Ashgate Publishing Limited.

Ayanwale, A. B. and Alimi, T. (2004), Microfinancing as a poverty alleviation measure: A gender analysis, Journal of Social Sciences, Vol. 9, N. 2, pp. 111-117.

Baum, J., Calabrese, T. and Silverman, B.S. (2000), Don't go it alone: Alliance networks and start-ups performance in Canadian Biotechnology, *Strategic Management Journal*, Vol. 21, pp. 276-294.

Chell, E. (2007), Social Enterprise and Entrepreneurship: Towards a Convergent Theory of the Entrepreneurial Process, *International Small Business Journal*, Vol. 25, N. 1, pp. 5-26.

Chen, B. and Krauskopf, J. (2011). Integrated or Disconnected? Examining Formal and Informal Networks in a Merged Nonprofit Organization", *Proceedings of the 2011 Annual Meeting of the Academy of Management*.

Franciscus, J., Koppenjan, M. and Klijn, E.H. (2004), Summing Up: Dealing with uncertainties in networks, *Managing Uncertainties in Networks: A Network Approach to Problem Solving*, Chp 6., pp. 113-130, .Routledge.

Hartungi, R. (2007), Understanding the success factors of micro-finance institution in a developing country, *International Journal of Social Economics*, Vol. 34, N. 6, pp.388 – 401.

Khandelwal, A.K. (2007), Microfinance Development Strategy for India, Economic and Political Weekly, Vol. 42, No. 13, pp. 1127 – 1135.

Morton, M., (1997), *SD Helps Revitalize Credit Unions in Africa*, Office of Sustainable Developments--A News Letter, Bureau for Africa, USAID, Fall/Winter, 1997.

Murisa, T. and Chikweche, T. (2012), Enterpreneurship and micro-finance in extreme poverty circumstances – challenges and prospects: The case of Zimbabwe, Journal of Development Entrepreneurship, Vol. 18, Issue 1,

Nader, Y.F. (2008), Micro-credit and the socio-economic wellbeing of women and their families in Cairo, The Journal of Socio-Economics, Vol. 37, Issue 2, pp. 644-656.

Nonaka, I. and Takeuchi, H. (1995), *The Knowledge Creating Company: how Japanese companies create the dynamics of innovation*, New York: Oxford University Press.

Taifi, N. and Gharbi, K. (2013), *IT integration in Strategic Management: The case of a micro-financing network*, In: Torres-Coronas, T. and Vidal-Blasco, M-A (eds), *Sociel e-Enterprise: Value creation through ICT*, chp 14, pp. 263-279.

Roubos, K. (2008), The Rise of Cross-Sector Partnerships in Microfinance: Environmental Causes and Future Potential, *Stanford Journal of Microfinance*, Vol. 1.

Sapovadia, V.K. (2006), Micro-Finance: The pillars of a tool to socio-economic development, Development Gateway, Vol. 6, pp. 34-37.

Shan, W., Walker, G. and Kogut, B. (1994), Inter-firm cooperation and start-up innovation in the biotechnology industry, *Strategic Management Journal*, Vol. 15, N. 55, pp. 387-394.

Symon, G. (2000), Information and communication technologies and the network organization: A critical analysis, *Journal of Occupational and Organizational Psychology*, Vol. 73, N.4, pp. 389–414.

Tidd, J. (2012), From knowledge management to strategic competences: Assessing technological, market, and organizational innovation, *Series on Technology Management*, Vol. 19., Worldscinet publising.

Tiwana, A. and McLean. E.R., (2005), Expertise Integration and Creativity in Information Systems Development, *Journal of Management Information Systems*, Vol. 22, N. 1, pp. 13-43.

Yoshino, M.Y. and Rangan, U.S (1995), *Strategic alliances: An enterpreneurial approach to globalization*. Harvard Business School Press, Boston.

Author Biography:

 **Nouha Taifi** is Assistant Professor in Management in Industrial Engineering Department, Mohammedia School of Engineers, Mohammed V University in Rabat, Morocco. She is also the Coordinator of the R&D Laboratory in ATTADAMOUNE MICRO-FINANCE, Fez, Morocco. She has various publications in the field of Micro-Financing Environment.

Model for Creating Sustainable Brands Through Managing Knowledge and Relational Capital

Ass. Prof. Slavica Trajkovska[1], Prof. Dr. Angelina Taneva-Veshoska[1], Kristina Antikj Georgievski[1] and Slobodan Trajkovski[2],
[1]Institute for Research in Environment, Civil Engineering and Energy, N. Macedonia
[2]Civil Engineering Institute MACEDONIA, JSC Skopje, N. Macedonia,
slavica.trajkovska@iege.edu.mk
angelina@iege.edu.mk
kristina@iege.edu.mk
slobodan.trajkovski@gim.mk

Abstract: This case serves as proof of the importance of managing knowledge and intellectual capital, providing special focus on managing the relational capital in companies. Crucial aspect in managing intellectual capital is nurturing the relations that the company has with its external and internal stakeholders. The case presents the RE-CAP© model, providing insight on the process of assessment of relational capital, establishing and nurturing relations, developing system for monitoring the implemented activities and setting up indicators, and providing digital tools to make this process easier and more efficient. Now as many companies are pursing the internal transformation toward digital transition and many internal processes need to be re-considered strategically and systematically. The RE-CAP© model has an innovative and practical approach to managing relational capital and marketing mix elements. It is result from an applied research project which IECE and CEIM conducted in the last two years. The model leverages marketing channels and relationships with external stakeholders, including clients, partners, and collaborators, to achieve a competitive advantage, enhance market value, increase productivity, and drive high business performance. By applying measurement tools, analysis techniques, and management strategies, the RE-CAP© model aims to uncover the value and potential of relational capital and utilise this knowledge to develop sustainable procedures and marketing solutions that promote long-term business growth. The RE-CAP© model can be replicated to other companies, adapting the indicators according to the company needs, the sector in which the company operates, setting the system in alignment with their strategic position. Incorporating the management of relational capital in the digitalised system in the organisation is an asset of the company which brings results in short and long term, making the organisation of the company more competitive, smartly using their contacts and their relations and having an impact on the brand towards more sustainable.

Keywords: *Sustainable Brand, Digitalisation, Relational Capital, Intellectual Capital, Knowledge Management, Organisational Capital.*

1. Introduction

This case serves as proof of the importance of managing knowledge and intellectual capital (IC), providing special focus on managing the relational capital (RC) in companies. Crucial aspect in managing intellectual capital is nurturing the relations that the company has with its external and internal stakeholders.

The RE-CAP© presented in this paper resulted from the applied research project "Creating model for managing relational capital and development of marketing solutions for sustainable brands" which started in 2021. The research project is organised by the Institute for Research in Environment, Civil Engineering and Energy (IECE) and the Civil Engineering Institute MACEDONIA JSC Skopje (CEIM). IECE and CEIM have previously conducted another applied research about IC and knowledge management (KM), creating the CO-IN© Model and receiving recognition with the awarded case "Innovative model for development of learning organisations through KM and intellectual capital".

Evidence from research and practice continuously shows the importance of IC for each organisation, the value in managing the intangible assets which the organisation possesses. Effective management of IC requires ongoing effort to manage each capital (relational, human and organisational). This is a long-term process, where some investments may take time to produce tangible results, but ultimately will lead to competitive advantage and sustainable brands.

Relational capital is a component of intellectual capital, which focuses on the intangible value that the organisation's relationships with its stakeholders bring. The RC if managed properly builds a strong foundation for providing valuable resources and expertise, access to new technologies, materials, building and nurturing quality relations based on trust and loyalty, as well establishing partnerships and collaborations.

Relational capital contributes to the realisation of the company's goals, and includes elements such as the reputation and potential of the relations. In the case we consider both the external and internal stakeholders that one organisation has (Figure 1).

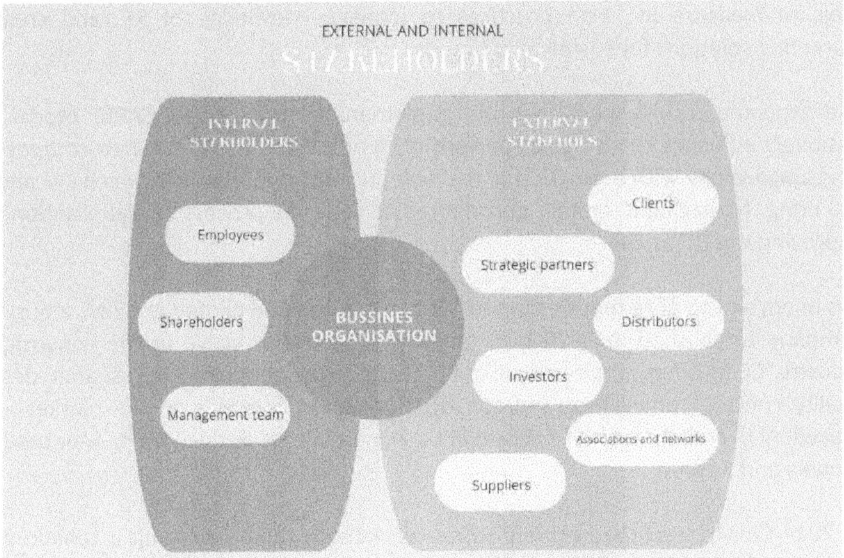

Figure 1: External and internal stakeholders

The intention of this research was to provide practical solutions how organisations can integrate sustainability in their business model (including all aspects – social, economic, environment, etc.).

The objectives of the research project are to:

- create a model for managing RC in order to increase the productivity and business performance of the organisation;
- set a system to monitor and evaluate the indicators for RC and support the decision-making process of the management creating reports;
- initiate strategic and systematic approach toward digitalisation of the process in the company enabling communication channels and flow of information;
- preserving the organisational memory and knowledge and information employees have related to the relevant stakeholders.

First, analysis of the existing models, research evidence and recommendations were taken in consideration, to continue finding answers to the questions related to types of stakeholders and their characteristics, quantitative and qualitative indicators and tools to measure RC, best practices to manage knowledge of RC, and creative marketing solutions for sustainable brands.

The expected results were that the implementation of the RE-CAP© Model will positively influence the business performance of the company and their competitive advantage, along with evaluation of the new business opportunities which KM and RC will bring. Managing IC and RC contributed to start the process of digitalisation and improving the OC as well.

It is important to note that this model was co-created and piloted in CEIM, a business company established in 1975 in Skopje, N. Macedonia, active in the construction industry. CEIM offers services in all areas of construction: planning, research, design, quality control, surveillance and construction. CEIM operates on the market in N. Macedonia, and through its subsidiaries regionally in: Serbia, B&H, Montenegro, Albania and Kosovo.

In 2014 CEIM established private research institute (IECE), creating a collaborative innovation partnership. This approach has been recognized by WEF, emphasizing the collaboration between young and established companies that share resources and combine efforts to support innovative ideas. CEIM and IECE developed the CO-IN model, as a holistic approach in university-industry collaboration in developing countries.

Their previous experience related to IC resulted in successfully transformed the company into a learning organisation, by setting up system for KM and IC. The need for implementing all the KM/IC activities were:

- more complex working conditions and aggravating factors and risks, both in the environment and in the constitution of the company
- the trend of encouraging development, research and innovation, as the main drivers of development in the modern global economy and the main strategic commitment of the European Union
- rapid technological development, rapid obsolescence of technologies and technological skills, the need for long-term planning to upgrade knowledge, which will have a longer use value
- competitiveness in the market, based on modern ways of corporate organisation, planning, management, operations and marketing

- phase of the life cycle in which the company is - reaching full maturity, which imposes the need to pursue goals and directions that will continue the upward trend of development, and will avoid stagnation and decline
- the company's tendency to expand more intensively on foreign markets

In this case we present the results after 2 years conducting the research project and the created RE-CAP© Model, along with the implemented activities, lessons learned and the next planned steps.

2. Infrastructure

The creation of the RE-CAP© model happened gradually, based on the several phases and activities:

- **Strategic approach** - Strategic positioning and system thinking creating strategic documents and setting business goals;
- **Analytical approach** - Analysis using desk and field research methods to understand the market, competition, external environment and internal environment and potential; and mapping the external and internal stakeholders and applying the VRIO model (assessing the uniqueness and value of the business offer);
- **Innovative approach** - Creating the RE-CAP© model and activities to stimulate and defining indicators and tools to monitor and evaluate aspects like relations, branding, clients, partnerships, marketing solutions; and initiating changes in the organisational structure such as introducing new job positions and sectors;
- **Technical approach** - Starting the digitalisation transformation of the company and improving the KM system.

2.1   Strategic approach

To start the process of managing knowledge and relational capital it is required to have strategic and systemic thinking, which was communicated through the strategic documents and setting up the strategic goals for the next 5 years. All implemented activities were implemented in accordance with CEIM Strategies:

- Development strategy,
- Marketing Strategy and
- Knowledge Management Strategy.

The summary of the strategic goals of these documents are presented in Table 1.

Table 1: CEIM Strategic documents and their objectives

Development strategy	Marketing Strategy	KM Strategy
Building sustainable brand, maintaining reputation in the business and social spheres	Managing relations of external and internal stakeholders	Detection (mapping) of knowledge in CEIM (basic level, advanced level, specific knowledge, research potential)
Maintaining a competitive advantage in the domestic market	Improving the branding of the company and the promotional materials	
Expanding the operations in markets in other countries	Organisation of events to positively stimulate team management and cooperation	Lack or need for certain knowledge (training plan and professional development
Improving financial performance	Improving organisational culture and internal communication	
Advancing existing services	Conducting analysis of the market and competition	Sharing, creating and retaining knowledge
Development of new services	Continuous presentation of the company, achievements and opportunities to the public	Organisational memory
Strengthening the capacities and nurturing the HR	Identification of potential partners and collaborators	Managing external knowledge networks and infrastructure
Continuity in investments	Establishing a system for price strategy	

2.2   Analytical approach

In the process of building an innovative model for managing knowledge and relational capital it is important to understand the current situation and analyse the future trends in the sector. For this purpose, a number of analyses were conducted using desk and field research methods to understand the market, competition, external environment (PESTEL analysis), internal environment and potential (SWOT and TOWS analysis). To get insight what is the unique value proposition of the company, its resources and services the VRIO model was applied. Additionally, extensive mapping of all relevant stakeholders (both internal and external) was done, assessing the relationship with each of them, previous joint activities, the length of relationship, motivation to cooperate, previous experiences, etc. Relationship mapping is helpful for organisations to acquire new customers, maintain the current relationships and partnerships and support the process of decision-making when new relationships are being built.

The results from this phase were a base to propose a series of measures and activities to improve resources in relational capital and successfully manage knowledge toward reaching the goal of becoming sustainable brand.

2.3   Innovative approach

In this phase we created the RE-CAP© model and proposed a set of activities to support managing the relational capital. One of the crucial activities was defining non-financial indicators connecting them with adequate tools in order to monitor and evaluate aspects of relational capital: relationships, corporate branding and identity, clients, partnerships, marketing solutions. This also initiated changes in the organisational structure, where two new sectors were established and new job position on management level was introduced.

The Relational Capital Management Model - RE-CAP© model has an innovative and practical approach to managing relational capital and marketing mix elements. The model leverages marketing channels and relationships with external stakeholders, including clients, partners, and collaborators, to achieve a competitive advantage, enhance market value, increase productivity, and drive high business performance.

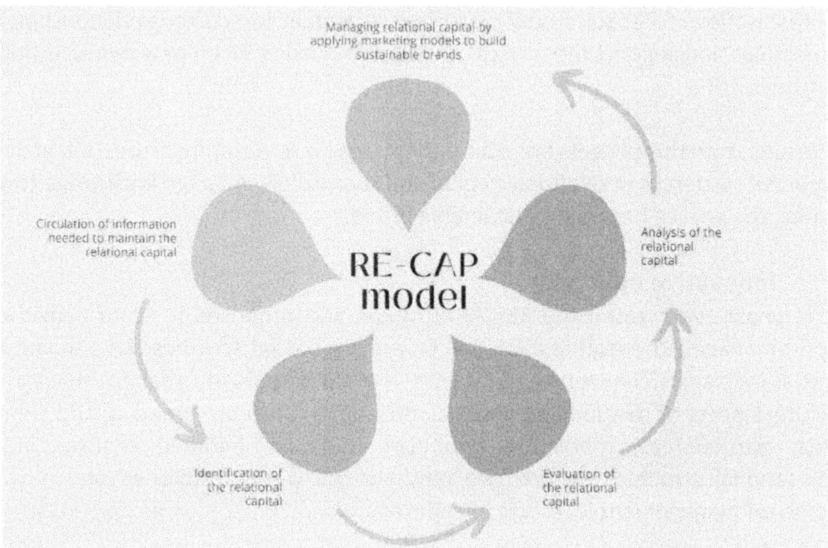

Figure 2: The RE-CAP© model

By applying measurement tools, analysis techniques, and management strategies, the RE-CAP© model aims to uncover the value and potential of relational capital and utilise this knowledge to develop sustainable procedures and marketing solutions that promote long-term business growth.

The goal of the model is using set of tools and indicators in a systematic way to increase the potential of the relational capital of one organisation. The information and knowledge created and shared will support the management staff in their strategic and operational tasks.

2.4   Main features of the RE-CAP© model are:

- Identification of the relational capital by creating a data base, containing all necessary information about the stakeholders;
- Evaluation of the relational capital using the defined quantitative and qualitative indicators set in relation with the strategic objectives of the company and annual targets;
- Analysis of the relational capital providing recommendation to the management staff whether to pursue a partnership, how to strengthen and

keep high quality of relation, trust and loyalty, initiate participations in networks, etc.;

- Managing relational capital by applying marketing models and creating innovative marketing solutions, such as events management, branding activities, etc.;
- Circulation of information needed to maintain the relation capital by enabling communication channels and flow, as well as storing the organisational memory connected to relational capital certain employees have.

Sample of the defined quantitative and qualitative indicators is presented in the following figure.

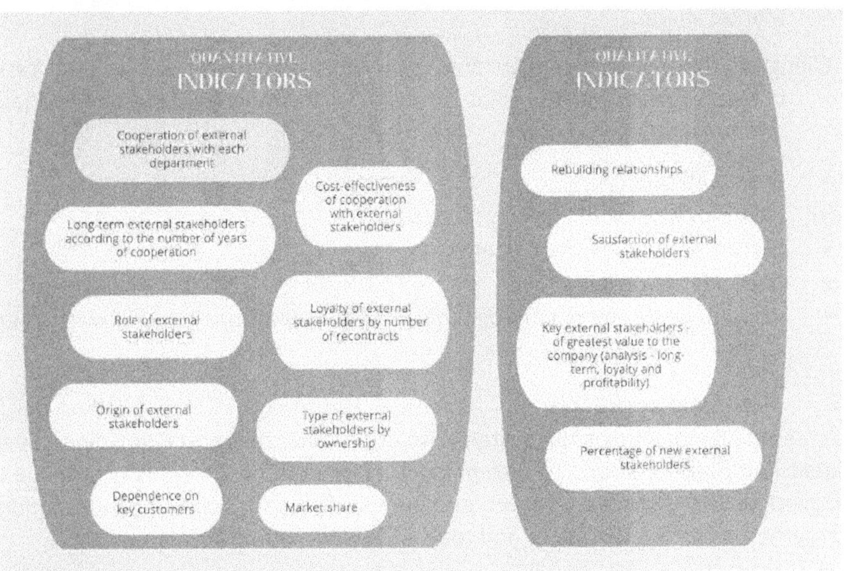

Figure 3: Quantitative and qualitative indicators of RC

There are three dimensions of relational capital which are taken in consideration:

Network capital - including all external stakeholders, in addition to customers with whom the company interacts and the relationships established. This dimension can be observed through the following aspects:

- Length / duration of the contact / relationship

- Type of relation / Strength of the relationship,
- The depth of the relationship at the organisational level,
- Quality of relationship with suppliers, delivery time,
- The network of suppliers and selection of an appropriate supplier
- Percentage of business partnerships or collaborations.

Brand capital - related to the company's position in the market and its competitive advantage, observed by the following aspects:

- Brand reputation and brand knowledge and awareness through market research,
- Brand image and brand marketing,
- Market share.

Client capital - especially important, is considered to be the key to a successful business. These relationships, are crucial in understanding and managing relational capital:

- Client satisfaction,
- Client loyalty, frequency of purchases,
- Percentage of new clients per year,
- Dependence on key clients
- Percentage of complaints or remarks and suggestions for improving clients' service.

2.5   Technical approach

After the development of the systemic solution and creation of the model it was evident that there is a need to systematically store and manage this knowledge and information. The first step was created new templates for collecting information or improving the current templates and tools.

The next phase was this process is digitalisation transformation of the company and improving the KM system. This process of transformation was already initiated last year, conceptualising the whole system, and this year is dedicated to developing technical solution. Next year is planned to start using the digital system and monitor the improvements in the management of IC and RC.

3. Challenges

Building an innovative model for transformation and development of sustainable brand is far from easy and smooth. It requires strategic and systemic thinking of the management team and understanding that it is a long-term process and the benefits from it can be observed after few years. Another important trait in this process is having a vision and leadership skills, because this process implies changes and need for transformation, which in many cases is objected and not welcomed. Very positive in this experience is the visionary leadership of the owners and the Supervisory board. Their support was crucial in addressing the challenges and overcoming them.

The initiative of creating sustainable brands through managing knowledge and relational capital is part of the bigger vision for managing knowledge and intellectual capital. Aligned with the strategic documents, CEIM introduced integrated business plan where elements of IC are incorporated.

Some of the challenges that were observed are:

- Change resistance – willingness to preserve old patterns, procedures and structures;
- Lack of time due to bad planning, too many obligations, motivation of managerial staff;
- Need for analysis and business insights in the industry;
- The intangible aspect of the process;
- Lot of information and knowledge stored in people, not in the system;
- Having hard time to see the bigger picture and effects due to everyday operational tasks.

The challenges were addressed accordingly and vigorously. The most effective and efficient way to tackle them was through communication and managing expectations.

Also, in order to overcome the challenges and create positive climate for the transformation toward learning organisation, many other activities were implemented:

- Investing more time in planning resources and projects;
- Events for creating positive organisational climate, with focus on collaboration and sharing;
- The lack of knowledge in the topic relational capital was tackled with presentations, reading materials and mentoring;
- Connecting relational capital with organisational capital which resulted in improving procedures, work positions, indicators and non-financial reports;

- Initiating a process of digitalisation in order to enable system to store information and knowledge;
- Change the organisational structure introducing two new sectors: Analytical centre and Centre for business and technological development;
- Opening new job positions of Sales directors who were assigned to manage relational capital with the external stakeholders.

4. How the initiative was received by the users

The initiative was gradually presented as the research project progressed. Several actions were implemented:

- Meetings with top management - Key to manage expectations were the frequent meetings with the top management board and the director for business and technological development.
- Presentation at the Business convention - The results from the first year were presented at the business convention, where presentation of progress to all managerial team (top and middle management staff) was done. Brainstorming and discussions were initiated in the direction of practical implementation of the model and the indicators and tools proposed.
- Introducing and implementing new system measures/ table improved/better reports - It was encouraging to see the feedback and engagement from several managers who embraced the process and improved templates they already used in order to measure certain indicators.
- New work tasks and responsibilities for some of the staff – New job role of Business directors (sales) specially dedicated to nurture the relational capital.
- Establishing the Analytical centre – with the intention to conduct analysis, systematically organising data and create reports to support the job of the Sales directors.

The initial use of the set indicators and tools already provided positive feedback related to better coordination, easier flow of information and preparation of reports and analysis.

Also, very positive comments and great satisfaction was observed by CEIM clients and partners, who communicated their impressions of healthy relations and stimulating organisational climate and distinctive organisational culture, which added more value and affirmation of the benefits of the whole transformational process.

5. The learning outcomes

The case presents the RE-CAP© model, providing insight on the process of assessment of relational capital, establishing and nurturing relations, developing system for monitoring the implemented activities and setting up indicators, and providing digital tools to make this process easier and more efficient. Now as many companies are pursing the internal transformation toward digital transition and many internal processes need to be re-considered strategically and systematically.

The lessons learned and changes made in this case are many. The most noticeable learning outcomes done are:

- Improvement of the organisational structure and the new job positions and sectors created;
- Setting up a system to measure quantitative and qualitative indicators;
- Creating integrated business plans which includes elements from IC;
- Connecting the management process with the marketing mix, creating solutions to manage RC;
- Embracing the digital transition and initiation a digital transformation in the company based on the IC management;
- Creating synergy between the strategic objectives and the tools and indicators with teams in relation to their job description and tasks.

In the following figure a sample of the distribution of tasks related to specific strategic objectives, targets and indicators is presented.

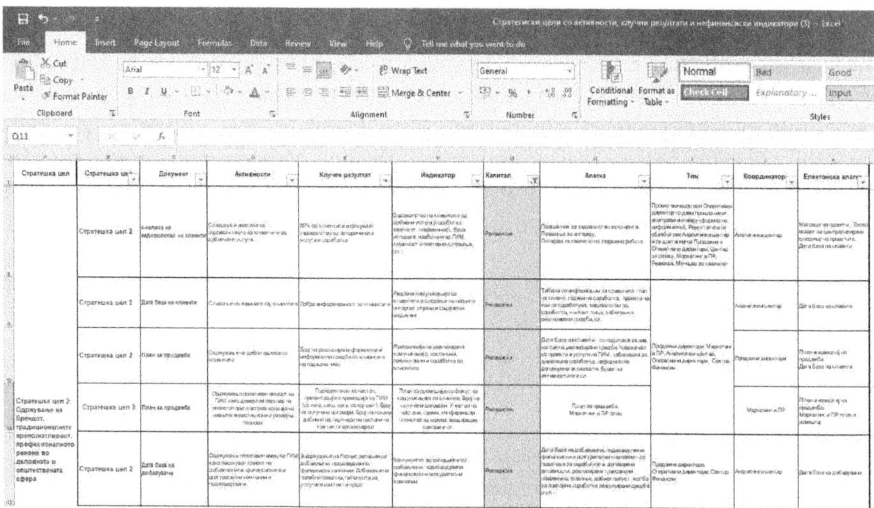

Figure 4: Overview of tasks and teams in relation to strategic objective and indicators

For example, for the Strategic goal Building sustainable brand, maintaining reputation in the business and social spheres several documents are prepared to analyse the progress, such as Sales plan, Data base of suppliers, Report on the satisfaction of clients, Data base of clients, etc. Specific key results are set for each of the indicators, specifying the tools to collect date, as well as the team and the team leader responsible for this task.

The perception from this process was evaluated and can be confirmed that the managerial staff positively values the management of RC. On the following table the results from the survey conducted with the management team are presented.

Table 2: Progress of the company in the last 5 years

Leadership in the industry	19%
Brand and image	22%
Future prospects for growth	25%
Response to the competition	29%
Rate of success of launching new services	8%
Overall business performance	10%
Increase of sales	15%
Increase of profit	21%
Market value of the company	20%

We can conclude that there is positive perception about the progress and development of the company. The results obtained are individual perception of the management team, and are not based on financial data. It can be observed that the managers see their company as flexible, being able to respond to the changes, with strong brand and prospects to growth.

On the following table the perception of several elements of relational capital are presented.

Table 3: Perception of progress on taken measures in relation to RC

Strategic partnerships and agreements	
The company works on joint projects with lot of other companies	32%
The company has different channels of distribution and cooperation	18%
The company is in a position to increase its value through collaboration and partnerships	19%
The strategic partnerships of the company influence the market value in a positive way	15%
Company brand and relations to clients and suppliers	
The marketing activities positively influence the brand of the company	30%
The clients prefer the company's service instead of the competitors	22%
There is a continuous monitoring on client's satisfaction	23%
Knowledge about the clients and suppliers	
The company receives feedback from the clients	12%
Knowing the clients and associates is on high level in the company	32%

The company is using useful and updated informational systems	22%

From the results it can be observed that there is a positive trend in the perception of the managerial staff in relation to several aspects of RC, especially regards the brand, marketing activities and the joint projects with strategic partners. However, it can be expected that as the digital system is implemented there will be increase in the perception of other aspects, such as receiving feedback from clients, market value and updated informational system.

Establishing a system for managing RC it is a long process, and should be done in a systematised way. We can conclude that there are many benefits from the RE-CAP© model, highlighting its approach, the systematic and practical solutions, the new digital system, the set of indicators to measure and report which leads to the effect of easier availability of information, better alignment of management team, flow of information on the stakeholders and increased performance.

6.   Plans to further develop the initiative

This case serves as proof and inspiration for companies, providing evidence of the positive effects on sustainable performance from managing RC and knowledge.

he RE-CAP© model can be replicated to other companies, adapting the indicators according to the company needs, the sector in which the company operates, setting the system in alignment with their strategic position. The positive effect for other companies is that the developed and implemented actions for RC can be replicated and further used by other organisations, motivated to enhance their development and sustainability-oriented performance. We have the intention to apply the model in other companies, and follow the need for adaptation of certain indicators and tools.

This model is built in a way so it can be scalable as well. It can be further improved and new elements added. The model proposes a set of actions and measures, has innovative approach to follow the progress, using quantitative and qualitative methods. Additionally, the investments in knowledge and RC are directly linked to increasing the competitive advantage of the organisation and their brand.

The future plans are to continue the development of the software tool, part of the digitalisation transformation. Incorporating the management of relational capital in the digitalised system in the organisation is an asset of the company which brings results in short and long term, making the organisation of the company more competitive, smartly using their contacts and their relations and having an impact on the brand towards more sustainable.

Also, another step which we plan is to offer education as support to the managerial team and to employees who participate in the implementation of the process.

The implications of the findings presented in this case are important from a practical perspective, as the information can assist managers to recognize the relevance of the topic and its importance, and support organisation development toward sustainability-oriented performance and brands. This case also provides practical implications in initiatives in RC, embedding sustainability in the strategy of the organisation and promoting awareness on the importance of sustainable business practices.

Author Biographies:

Ass. Prof. Slavica Trajkovska, PhD in Labour Economics, is the founder of IECE, private research institute, established to be center of excellence, supporting collaborative and innovative partnerships. She has more than 25 years of experience working in management and leadership positions, doing research and offering consultancy services in the field of intellectual capital, sustainable systems and brands.

Prof. Dr. Angelina Taneva-Veshoska, PhD in Management, is Director of IECE. Her research and teaching interests include Intellectual capital, Human capital, Sustainability, Business models. She has almost two decades of experience in managing educational and research projects, capacity building and business consultancy activities.

Kristina Antic Georgievski MA in Strategic Marketing and Strategic Management, is marketing manager in IECE and in Civil Engineering Institute Macedonia. Her working fields are in marketing sector including public relations, event management and sustainable brands. She has more than 15 years' experience in public relation, creating multiple events for different industries working with private sector in the domestic and international market.

 **Slobodan Trajkovski**, MA in Political Sciences, is the President of the Management Board in Civil Engineering Institute Macedonia. He has more than 10 years' experience in the company, working in the audit and analytics sector and in the procurement department. He is actively involved and supports investments in innovative and sustainable solutions for maintaining competitive brands.